Advanced Pra

"If you've ever wondered how you can make work and money decisions without second thoughts or blindly going with 'what seems good,' buy this book immediately. I wish I had known about the tips, strategies, and advice Roger lays out years ago when I was feeling lost as a corporate overachiever. *Work Your Money, Not Your Life* is an engaging read that reminds us that professional and financial success are in our control."

—Lauren McGoodwin, founder and CEO of Career Contessa

"Work Your Money, Not Your Life is the perfect book for anyone who wants their career to work for them instead of the other way around. It's a highly actionable read that doesn't just motivate you, but also helps you figure out exactly what to do in order to align your career and money with your values. It's a must-read for anyone who feels stuck in a job or unsatisfied with their career."

—Kristin Wong, author of *Get Money: Live the Life You Want, Not Just the Life You Can Afford*

"Candid, relatable, and funny, Roger draws on his unique background as a banker-turned-Googler and financial planner to help readers tackle their biggest stressors. This powerful read shows us how taking simple steps to master our money can enable us to build a meaningful career and achieve a fulfilling life."

—Nicole Lapin, author of *Rich Bitch* and *Boss Bitch*

"What's your most valuable asset? Most likely, it's you — and the paychecks you'll collect in the decades ahead. That's the starting point for Roger Ma's unique and enlightening book, which takes that hugely valuable asset and shows you how to turn it into the career and financial life you want. Your journey has the potential to be wonderful and enriching, especially with Roger as your guide."

—Jonathan Clements, editor of `HumbleDollar.com` and former personal finance columnist for *The Wall Street Journal*

Work Your Money,
Not Your Life

Work Your Money, Not Your Life

How to Balance Your Career and Personal Finances to Get What You Want

Roger Ma
with Jennifer Ma

WILEY

Published by John Wiley & Sons, Inc., Hoboken, New Jersey.
Published simultaneously in Canada.

For general information on our other products and services or for technical support, please contact our Customer Care Department within the United States at (800) 762–2974, outside the United States at (317) 572–3993, or fax (317) 572–4002.

Wiley publishes in a variety of print and electronic formats and by print-on-demand. Some material included with standard print versions of this book may not be included in e-books or in print-on-demand. If this book refers to media such as a CD or DVD that is not included in the version you purchased, you may download this material at http://booksupport.wiley.com. For more information about Wiley products, visit www.wiley.com.

Library of Congress Cataloging-in-Publication Data

Names: Ma, Roger (Financial planner), author.
Title: Work your money, not your life : how to balance your career and personal finances to get what you want / Roger Ma ; with Jennifer Roberts Ma.
Description: Hoboken, NJ : John Wiley & Sons, Inc., [2020] | Includes index.
Identifiers: LCCN 2019050437 (print) | LCCN 2019050438 (ebook) | ISBN 9781119600367 (paperback) | ISBN 9781119600381 (ePDF) | ISBN 9781119600374 (ePub)
Subjects: LCSH: Finance, Personal. | Saving and investment.
Classification: LCC HG179 .M1655 2020 (print) | LCC HG179 (ebook) | DDC 332.024—dc23
LC record available at https://lccn.loc.gov/2019050437
LC ebook record available at https://lccn.loc.gov/2019050438

COVER ART & DESIGN: PAUL McCARTHY

Printed in the United States of America

VC6877F1F-70AE-4313-ACA8-CF67A9D3E948_022820

Contents

Introduction

On paper, everything seemed to be falling into place for me. I was in my late 20s, living in the center of Manhattan, thriving at a top investment bank, dining at Michelin-starred restaurants, and traveling to stunning international destinations. This is why I had worked so hard through high school and college – to be able to live this "dream life." But on the inside, something didn't feel right.

Work and money were at the heart of my struggles, despite the fact that I had what was considered a "good" job and ample savings. Most mornings, I'd hear my alarm and dread having to go into the office. My hours were long and unpredictable, often stretching into the late evenings, some early mornings, and most weekends. The grueling schedule meant missing friends' birthday parties, cancelling dates, and having little time to relax or recharge.

The actual nuts and bolts of my job were far from being glamorous. Even worse, the work I did on a day-to-day basis didn't align with my interests. This was definitely not how I had imagined my career unfolding. But ironically, at the same time that I was trying to figure out how to right the ship and change my situation, others were reaching out to me for advice on how to get on the same path I was on — leaving me confused about what, if anything, I should do to improve my job.

When it came to personal finance, I was no better off. As the child of immigrant parents, I had always been good at saving (sometimes to an extreme), and I certainly wasn't living paycheck to paycheck. Yet money stressed the heck out of me. In fact, any time I wasn't doing work, I was probably freaking out about some aspect of my finances. Along the way, I made all of the textbook money mistakes.

For starters, I was overwhelmed easily. I remember looking blankly at the 25 different investment options available in my 401(k) plan, without the faintest idea of how to even begin figuring out my investment strategy. After agonizing over the decision for months, I decided to throw in the towel and simply put my money equally into four mutual funds that "sounded good."

I also sought financial guidance from the wrong people, like when I would listen to talking heads on TV to get clues on the direction of the stock market. Even worse, I'd use their often inaccurate predictions to time when I should move my money around. In short, rather than being in control of my finances, I let my finances control me.

Over the last decade, I've gradually made the necessary changes to pave a path that fits my interests, skills, and priorities. Today, I balance a rewarding career at Google with running a financial planning firm that helps others address the same concerns about money that I once faced. I finally feel at peace with both my career and finances.

But the process to get to where I am now certainly wasn't easy. Initially, I was scared to take action and experiment; and once I got going, I failed often. In retrospect, I realize that a lot of my struggles stemmed from viewing my professional and financial needs as isolated parts of my life, rather than two intertwined pieces. Through my work as a financial planner, I see that many of my clients also struggle to reconcile these two issues. I'm guessing that since you're reading this book, you might be in the same situation.

This book is the resource I wish I had in my 20s as I fumbled through trying to optimize my career and finances. Over the course of my writing, I consulted with a variety of experts on work and money who generously shared their insights, including career strategists, financial planners, entrepreneurs, Fortune 500 executives, motivational speakers, recruiters, life coaches, journalists, and bestselling authors. I also delved deep into the research on career and financial issues to look for common threads. All the while, I tried to connect my own journey and those of my financial planning clients with what I had learned from others.

While career and money issues are intrinsically linked, I recognize that a book combining these subjects is not exactly a beach read. In order to cover both topics without making you want to jump in front of a car, I've only provided the information you need to know to see the big picture and take action, rather than bogging you down with all of the minute details. In addition to introducing concepts to you, this book will occasionally use stories from my own or other people's experiences. Although the stories are based on actual events, certain details, such as the names of people, groups, and companies, may have been changed to maintain the privacy of the individual and/or not disclose confidential information.

Consider yourself warned, however, that this book is an *active* read. In particular, I'll be asking you to answer some questions about your needs and values that you might need to think long and hard about. I'll also provide you with a series of exercises focused on your career and financial situations. I encourage you to put in the time to do this legwork so that you can create a truly customized roadmap for achieving your goals.

I hope you find this book helps you balance your professional and financial decisions for greater stability, satisfaction, and peace. While the road ahead may not always be easy, I can assure you that the payoff is worth it. Because you *can* work your money, not your life.

Now let me show you how.

Part I

Here's the Deal

"Not everything that counts can be counted, and not everything that can be counted counts."

– Albert Einstein

I'm sure you're eager to jump into the actual nuts and bolts of optimizing your career and finances. But before concerning ourselves with any practical details or fancy arithmetic, let's take a step back and identify *why* the work we'll be doing together in this book is important.

Although work and money are interconnected, the extent to which these two areas of our lives impact and inform each other may not be so obvious. It certainly wasn't to me. However, I've found that creating an integrated work and money strategy can empower people to gain more control over their lives than they might have imagined, leading to greater happiness and a clearer sense of purpose. This has certainly been the case for many of my financial planning clients, as well as for me personally.

We'll cover several key concepts in this section that will help motivate you on your journey toward professional and financial well-being. In particular, we'll examine how your living expenses can either help or hurt your job and life flexibility. We'll also clear up some common misconceptions about how to pursue a satisfying career by dispelling several of the myths that may have led us into unrewarding jobs. The insights you gain will lay the foundation for your work and money plan.

Chapter 1
You're Worth More Than You Think

Since you're reading this book, chances are that you can relate to my story in some way. Maybe you have what is considered a "good" job by most standards, yet you feel like you don't have much to show for it. Your net worth seems to be growing slowly, or not at all, and may even be negative ... and to make matters worse, it's not like you hop out of bed in the morning skipping to work. Or maybe you love your career, but you can't figure out how to meet your financial goals. At times you may wonder, "What am I doing all this for? I imagined life to turn out a little differently than this."

You're not alone. Nearly 70% of Americans don't like their jobs, according to a Gallup study,[1] and 65% of Americans lose sleep over their financial worries, based on a CreditCards.com poll.[2] Career and money woes appear to be especially prevalent among young professionals. In fact, a LinkedIn survey found that 75% of people in their 20s and 30s had experienced "insecurity and doubt" around work and money (no duh, right?) — or what they might call a "quarter-life crisis."[3]

While many of us have tried to improve our careers and our finances, we may have done so by approaching them as two totally separate problems. But in reality, decisions you make in one of these

3

areas can have a huge impact on all other areas of your life. When I came to this realization for myself, it totally changed how I thought about work and money, and how I chose to live my life.

Net Worth Is Not the Be-All and End-All

"You are not your job, you're not how much money you have in the bank. You are not the car you drive. You're not the contents of your wallet."[4]

Yeah, that's a line from the movie *Fight Club,* but it's true: your net worth doesn't define who you are as a person or equate to your self-worth. Yet, early in my career, that's exactly what I thought. It was a pretty demoralizing mindset, especially when I stacked myself up against the billionaire corporate titans who graced the covers of *Forbes* and *Fortune.*

I was so focused on the dollars and cents (or lack thereof) that I neglected to account for everything else I had going for me. I was a young, college-educated professional with plenty of time to build my skills and earnings potential — my human capital. And according to the College Board, the value of your human capital can be significant, with average lifetime earnings for a college graduate estimated at nearly $1.2 million.[5] Unfortunately, human capital isn't an asset that is typically accounted for in the calculations of a simple net-worth statement — but maybe it should be.

If you think about your total wealth as being made up of both your human and financial capital (Figure 1.1), it becomes clear how your work and money are connected, and why it's so important to find a job you like. In the beginning of our careers, our ability to work and earn income actually comprises the majority of our wealth. As we work, we begin to convert part of our earnings potential into real dollars, which allows us to fund our living expenses, save for our financial goals, and grow our financial net worth. During our prime working years, and especially early on, small improvements to our human capital, like building new skills or starting a side hustle, could have a much larger impact on our future net worth than trying to earn an extra 1% on our tiny investment portfolio.

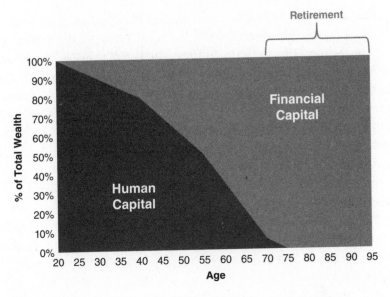

Figure 1.1   The evolution of your human and financial capital.

Saving Money Is About More Than Just Retirement

Do you ever think about how bizarre the concept of saving for retirement is? After finally getting out of school, you enter the workforce raring to start a real job (or if nothing else, to be getting a paycheck), only to immediately be told that you should start socking away money for retirement — a point that feels like eons into the future when you're supposed to just play golf, volunteer, and sit on the beach. What the heck?

The reason this sequence of events may sound odd is because there's nothing logical about retiring. In fact, retirement as we know it didn't even exist until the late nineteenth century, when a politically savvy German chancellor invented the concept. For all of recorded history up until that point, you worked until you died — usually in labor-intensive jobs.[6] Even when retirement programs did begin to gain popularity, workers couldn't begin collecting pensions until they were 65 or 70 years old. At the time, a lot of people died before they could even make it to retirement — and if they did make it, they often didn't get to enjoy it for long.

Fast forward to the present day, and it becomes clear that our attitudes about retirement haven't caught up with the times. The median retirement age in the United States today is 62,[7] despite the fact that life expectancies have leapt to the 80s.[8] Meanwhile, work has become much less physically taxing (gotta love the information superhighway!). While it would be tough for most 75-year-olds to toil at the steel mills all day, they might not find it so hard to consult for companies, write memos, or drive for Uber. And sure, playing golf and sitting on the beach sounds fun when you're working 60-hour weeks, but that could get old really quick (no pun intended).

Don't get me wrong — I do think saving for a potential retirement is important, but what if we could reframe our thinking about jobs, retirement, and this large financial goal? What if you could find a job that you loved doing, and that you didn't want to retire from? In that paradigm, you might still save money as early as possible in your career — but it wouldn't be solely to help fund your retirement. Instead, you could benefit from your good savings habits *immediately* by gaining greater flexibility to find a career you enjoy now, and even take some breaks along the way.

And get this: you don't need to amass a bajillion dollars before you can start doing this.

So, how much money do you need to gain more freedom and control over your life? That's your financial runway: the amount of savings needed to achieve your goals based on your specific situation, underlying expenses, and values.

How Long Is Your Runway?

A short financial runway is simply having an emergency fund — typically three to six months of living expenses saved in a checking or savings account. For example, if you spend $5,000 a month, you should build a target emergency fund of $15,000 to $30,000. Financial planners (myself included) usually recommend establishing an emergency fund as one of the first priorities for clients. This gives people a stash of money to tap in case something unexpected happens to them, whether that's losing your job, unforeseen health-care expenses, or some other costly emergency.

A really long financial runway is sometimes referred to as financial independence — a concept that has become particularly popular among millennials through the Financial Independence, Retire Early movement (some use the acronym FIRE for short). Financial independence is typically defined as no longer needing to work for money because your savings and the income from your investment portfolio are sufficient to cover your living expenses. Many in the personal finance community use the 4% rule as a start-ing point to measure financial independence — a rule of thumb that says people need 25 times their annual expenses saved across cash and investments to reach financial independence. Building on our example above, if you spend $5,000 a month (or $60,000 a year), to be considered financially independent, you would need to have $1.5 million in cash and investments ($60,000 × 25).

How Much Is Enough for Financial Independence? Understanding the 4% Rule

The classic calculation for determining how much you need to achieve financial independence is based on a series of studies. In 1994, financial planner Bill Bengen laid the foundation for the 4% rule by publishing research on how much people could safely withdraw from their retirement portfolios each year without running out of money.[9] Because the results varied based on the year people retired and the sequence of market returns they experienced, Bengen's study looked at how various investment portfolios would have fared for a 30-year retirement for start years of 1926 through 1975. His analysis found that people could safely withdraw 4% of their investment portfolio in the first year of

(continued)

(*continued*)

retirement, and 4% plus a cost-of-living adjustment in subsequent years. On a $1.5 million portfolio, that would mean being able to safely withdraw $60,000 in the first year of retirement. Subsequent research, including the well-known Trinity Study[10] conducted by a group of professors from Trinity University, confirmed Bengen's findings.

Thus, the 4% rule was born. From a mathematical perspective, you can calculate the amount of money you would need to reach financial independence by simply dividing your annual expenses by 4%. Because doing mental math with percentages is sometimes tricky, people typically simplify the formula by multiplying their annual expenses by 25. (4% is the mathematical equivalent of 4/100 and 1/25 — i.e., 100/4% = 100 × 25.)

While researchers determined that 4% was the safe withdrawal rate for a 30-year retirement, it's important to note that this is just a rule of thumb. In Bengen's study, there were several scenarios where people actually ended up with a lot of extra money left over. On the other hand, Bengen used market conditions and returns for a specific period of time — and as we know from investment commercials on TV, past performance does not necessarily indicate future results.

Breaking Free: The Power of Financial Runway

Whether you're looking to make some big change or just a subtle mental shift, having financial runway can give you the confidence and funding needed to take action, so you can improve the immediate and long-term quality of your life.

Let's start with job satisfaction. Increasing your financial runway can positively impact your work situation by expanding the types of jobs you can pursue and by providing you the flexibility to take more professional risks. In practice, that could mean being able to accept a lower-paying but more fulfilling role that better aligns with your interests. Or it could mean feeling confident in changing industries, despite needing to work your way up all over again. Or maybe you're burned out from work and need to take a break — in which case, financial runway could allow you to take that unpaid leave and travel the world.

Kristin Wong, author of *Get Money* and contributor to the *New York Times*, realized the power of financial runway early in her career. After graduating from college, she landed a technical writer role in which she created content for product manuals — not exactly her dream job. After doing a number of side gigs, she realized she wanted to try her hand at screenwriting. To facilitate her job transition, Wong spent a year stockpiling six months of financial runway.

"If I hadn't saved up that money, I never would have been able to move to Los Angeles without a job," Wong says. "It bought me the time I needed to land a writing job and pursue a career path that eventually led me to where I am now."

On a subtler level, financial runway can help improve your day-to-day state of mind — often in small but meaningful ways. My client Morgan, for example, suffered from major burnout after working for a couple years as an associate at a large law firm because of her demanding colleagues, heavy workload, and incessant reactive requests. Although she wanted to do a good job, she felt trapped and bitter — that is, until she learned about the concept of financial runway.

When Morgan reached 12 months of financial runway, something interesting happened — she began to feel a sense of freedom. Having that much financial runway set aside allowed Morgan to walk into work every day knowing she was *choosing* to be there, rather than feeling like she was trapped and had no say in the matter. Going to work empowered and with a more positive mindset had other benefits as well; for example, Morgan found herself more receptive to feedback, more tolerant of difficult co-workers, and more patient about her career progression.

The subtle changes that result from having financial runway can also translate into more concrete and long-term benefits. If you approach your job from a positive mental state, you may produce higher-quality work and get along better with your co-workers. Ultimately, these improvements can make you more valuable to your employer, which could lead to promotions and a higher salary — enabling you to further build your financial runway so that you can continue making choices that align with your goals and values. That's what I'm talking about!

Dreaming of Winning the Lottery

Back in my finance days, my co-workers and I had a tradition of pooling our money together whenever the lottery jackpot reached at least $300 million. With the money everyone chipped in, we'd buy a bunch of tickets to improve our odds of winning. In the unlikely chance that we did win something, we knew we'd take the money upfront — so on a $300 million jackpot, after splitting the winnings among 30 people, each of us would be left with about $2.5 million.

Often, for the rest of the day, many of us would dream about what we would do if we actually won the lottery. Much of what we said is probably what many people would do in that unlikely situation — quit our jobs, take a break from working, buy some real estate, get back in shape, and travel. In other words, we'd live the dream.

Alas, our team never did win the jackpot. After each drawing, all of us would reluctantly go back to work and continue to grind out another day. Perhaps more unfortunate was the fact that many of us felt that the only way to live a life we wanted was by winning the lottery.

You *Can* Take Back Control of Your Life

Although it sounds counterintuitive, financial runway is primarily influenced by *how much you spend*, not by *how much you make*. Let that sit and marinate for a moment.

I always thought I needed to reach a certain income level or accumulate a massive amount of money before I could secure some buffer in my life. What I didn't realize was that controlling or decreasing my living expenses could actually make a large impact.

Consider two friends, John and Mark, who both make a gross salary of $150,000 and take home $100,000 after taxes. John has living expenses of $95,000 a year, while Mark lives on $60,000 a year.

By comparing their situations in Table 1.1, you can see how spending less allows you to:

- **Save money faster:** Because John spends most of his income, after a year of working, he isn't even able to save a month of financial runway. Meanwhile, Mark lives more frugally and saves eight months of financial runway over the same period of time.
- **Reduce the cost of certain goals:** Interestingly, because John's expenses are higher, he also has to save more money on an absolute basis to bankroll an emergency fund ($23,750 vs. $15,000) and his retirement ($2.375 million vs. $1.5 million). The combination of his high expenses and low savings rate means it will take him nearly five years to simply fund a minimum emergency fund (i.e., three months of living expenses), while it takes Mark just 4.5 months to fund his minimum emergency fund.
- **Gain flexibility in job choices:** John is pretty much locked into his current job or roles that pay a similar salary. His expenses are such that if he made less money, he would be running up significant credit card debt. Mark, on the other hand, has a fair amount of flexibility. If Mark received a job offer at a salary of $100,000, he could accept the position if he wanted because his living expenses are low.

Table 1.1   How Living Expenses Can Impact Your Career and Life Flexibility.

	John	Mark
Gross Salary	$150,000	$150,000
Taxes	$50,000	$50,000
Net Pay	$100,000	$100,000
Expenses	$95,000	$60,000
Savings/Year	$5,000	$40,000
Financial Runway/Year	0.63 Months	8 Months
Emergency Fund Needed	$23,750	$15,000
Time to Fund Emergency Fund	57 Months	4.5 Months
Retirement Savings Needed	$2,375,000	$1,500,000
Minimum Salary Needed	$150,000	$90,000

The bottom line is, your expenses have a *huge* impact on the amount of flexibility you can have, the cost of your financial goals, and the types of jobs you can take.

You Don't Need to Be Financially Independent to Have Financial Flexibility

Take a moment to think about your career, finances, and overall life. What type of pain points do you deal with on a daily basis? How would you feel if you could eliminate these frictions from your life? How much financial runway would you need to be able to do so?

Regardless of how you answered those questions, I have some good news: you likely don't need to be financially independent to have flexibility or freedom to change your career and life for the better. In fact, the amount of financial runway you'll need could be as little as a three-month emergency fund. The exact number will depend on the nature of the personal or professional change you're looking to make, whether you have a partner or parent who can help bridge the gap in living expenses (if necessary), and your own personal risk tolerance.

The first step toward determining the amount of financial runway you need is to gauge your current job and financial situation, which you'll be doing in Part 2. Then, you'll complete a series of exercises to identify attributes of your ideal career path. The more dissimilar your current and target jobs are, the larger your financial cushion will likely need to be to facilitate a switch. If you can continue to work in your current job and build the skills or experience needed to pivot to your ideal role, you may need less financial runway.

Your Ideal Career Is Within Reach

I hope that the concepts we've covered in this chapter have convinced you that you're worth more than a simple net worth statement. Regardless of your particular situation, the combined effect of your human capital and your ability to build financial runway means that real change is possible in your career — even if you're starting with a negative net worth and have loads of student loans to pay off.

In the next chapter, we'll take a deep dive into understanding why so many of us feel trapped in our jobs despite being able to tap our human capital and financial runway. I'll challenge you to reconsider certain beliefs that you may have subconsciously internalized, allowing you to move toward the career *you* want instead of a path that society has laid out for you.

Chapter 2

Everything You've Been Taught About Jobs Is Wrong

"More is better."
"Everyone has a calling."
"It's called work for a reason."

Do these sayings sound familiar? They're just a few of the countless messages we're bombarded with on a daily basis about what constitutes a "good" job and life. But with so many of us dreading the arrival of Monday mornings, maybe the lessons we've been taught have been wrong all along.

You might know what it's like to work in a "good" job, only to feel miserable doing it. Thinking something like, "This is it?" can put us into a vicious cycle of continuing to aspire for more – a higher salary, a more prestigious job title, a bigger house, and a nicer car – at the expense of our other needs, which then may make us even more dissatisfied. I know because I did this for years.

My story isn't unique. I spent much of my 20s chasing after the job myths that I'd been fed instead of what I truly valued. If I happened to achieve any of the traditional career milestones, like getting a good bonus, a nice pay raise, or a promotion, it would put a smile on my face for a couple of weeks and I'd indulge in a blow-out dinner or a few fancy ties. But pretty soon, life would normalize again – which meant I was back to grinding out my job and worrying about my next performance review instead of addressing some more important questions, like why the heck I was working so hard in the first place.

The problem stemmed from the fact that I had subscribed to many falsehoods about career success without knowing it. Even when I did finally realize the errors of my ways, I struggled to correct my job situation because I made the mistake of replacing one myth with another. While several of these messages seemingly contradicted one another, they all shared the same basic premise: you can only solve for happiness or money. Now I know better.

Let's dispel several of the myths that have held me back at various points in my career, and which might also be preventing you from finding the right path.

"It's All About Money and Prestige"

I remember a classmate asking me in third grade what my dad's job title was and how much money he made. Unfortunately, Take Your Child to Work Day didn't exist back then, so I had no idea. Besides, I was too busy organizing my baseball card collection to concern myself with such pedestrian matters. But that exchange left an impression on me that money and prestige were what mattered in your career.

I wasn't entirely wrong, of course. Money *is* important. We all need some amount of cash to fund our living expenses, after all. And wanting money isn't a bad thing, either. As business theorist Clay Christensen explains in his book *How Will You Measure Your Life?*, "The point isn't that money is the root cause of professional unhappiness. It's not. The problems start occurring when it becomes the priority over all else, when hygiene factors are satisfied but the quest remains only to make more money."[1]

The scenario Christensen describes is exactly what I experienced as a young banker. During those years, I thought – wrongly – that if my salary and bonus didn't make me feel like a million bucks, maybe I just needed to work harder and earn even higher figures. But in reality, I was playing a losing game by having fallen into the trap of thinking more was better. In the years since, I've seen a number of my clients make the same mistake.

So what *really* makes people happy? One of the most famous theories comes from American psychologist Abraham Maslow, who in 1943 proposed that all humans have specific needs that can be depicted as a five-level, pyramid-shaped hierarchy[2] (see Figure 2.1). After your basic needs are met, we move on to needs at the higher tiers of the pyramid – including love, prestige, and self-actualization. While many other studies have subsequently been conducted on human needs and happiness, they generally draw the same conclusion: solving for *only* security and financials will leave you unfulfilled. That's what causes the empty "Is this it?" feeling that keeps us on a hamster wheel.

Even though I experienced that empty feeling over and over again while working in investment banking, I was scared to make a transition because I thought it would be like throwing in the towel and giving up – going against all that I had been taught about success and happiness. In fact, I might never have willingly changed paths were it not for the fact that change happened to *me*: after working in the industry for seven years while climbing the corporate ladder, I unexpectedly lost my job as part of a mass layoff.

Although this turn of events was scary and uncomfortable, it gave me the time and space to redefine what a good job meant to me. With a lot of encouragement from my girlfriend (now wife) and friends, I was gradually able to shift my mindset and deprioritize money and prestige as being the most important aspects of a job. As a result, I finally did transition to another type of work that better aligned with my worldview, while adding on a side hustle in personal finance that could satisfy my entrepreneurial instincts.

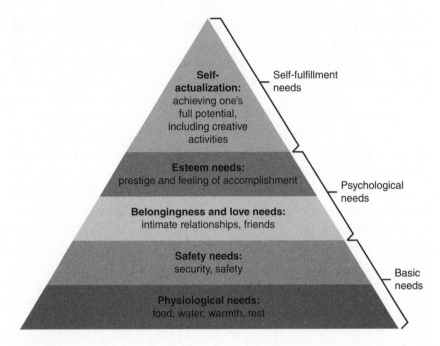

Figure 2.1 Maslow's hierarchy of needs

Now whenever I need to make a big decision about my career, I play back a line in my head from the movie *Moneyball* to remind myself of what I learned during my banking years. In the scene, baseball team executive Billy Beane (played by Brad Pitt) says, "I made one decision in my life based on money and I swore I would never do it again."[3] Ditto Brad Pitt, ditto.

"The Goal of Working Is to Climb the Corporate Ladder"

Early in my professional life, I believed that careers were linear – that is, you would pay your dues in a junior-level role, hone your skills, and eventually work your way up to the top. Sounds logical, right? After all, everyone says the goal of working is to climb the corporate ladder.

I looked to my colleagues a couple of years ahead of me as a model for my future progression, thinking my compensation package and standard of living would follow their path. In finance speak, I was trying to use past performance to predict future results, which isn't a guarantee in any facet of our lives – including in our careers.

I've come to realize that my assumptions as a fresh-out-of-college professional are shared by many. While we may think careers are supposed to move in a linear fashion, they typically do not – nor should they. In fact, people who get the most out of their careers often take routes that look more like zigzags rather than straight lines. Their paths may include taking breaks, switching industries, taking a step back, or accepting a pay cut – a process that allows them to grow their skills, better understand their interests, and increase their career satisfaction.

Take Adam Liptak, Supreme Court reporter for the *New York Times*. Liptak's distinguished career of more than three decades has been anything but linear. After law school, he spent four years as a litigation associate at a top law firm. But instead of embarking on the traditional path to law firm partner, Liptak decided to take a different route by transitioning to an in-house attorney role, and eventually becoming a legal reporter. Had Liptak restricted himself to *only* opportunities that resulted in higher pay, a title increase, or other traditional external measures of a "good" job, his career path would have looked very different, and he might have felt much less fulfilled.

"Each career move I made required me to take a cut in pay, but each role was more satisfying and made me happier than the previous job," Liptak says. "From a purely financial standpoint, I suppose I made stupid choices. But life is not purely financial."

Liptak's story illustrates that the working world can be more unpredictable than many career books paint it. You don't always have to earn higher salaries or promotions every year. In fact, trying to do so may create artificial barriers around which opportunities you can take and prevent you from increasing your career satisfaction.

When you open your eyes to opportunities that do not follow a traditional path, you may need to take a pay cut in the short term. But with sufficient financial runway, those moves can be feasible – allowing you to find work you're passionate about and possibly increase your long-term career earnings.

"Everyone Has One True Calling"

The saying that everyone has one true calling is another myth, and a dangerous one at that. In my mid-20s, when I would window-shop other roles outside of finance, many positions sounded interesting, but not like "calling" material. So I would stop my explorations there – short-changing myself out of learning about other options that, in retrospect, could have helped inform my career path.

I'm not alone. The myth of the calling often leads people on a treasure hunt to try to find "the one" – an ideal job that doesn't actually exist. The truth is, someone may have many different passions that they wish to pursue over the course of their lives, or even concurrently.

Bestselling author and Grammy-winning producer Kabir Sehgal is one such person. Instead of trying to find that needle in a haystack, Sehgal has worked in as many as four different jobs at the same time. He has frequently paired more traditional roles, including the positions of navy officer, investment banker, and corporate strategist, with creative pursuits, like writing books and composing and producing music.

"Two careers are better than one," says Sehgal. "Committing to two careers allows you to follow your curiosities and potentially feel more fulfilled. As I discovered, you may also end up doing both jobs better than if you only had one role."

While you don't have to keep pace with Sehgal by picking up three more jobs, you also shouldn't feel pressured to find a single role that fulfills *all* of your needs. That's why later in this book, we'll be devoting an entire chapter to how you can pursue a side hustle.

"Do What You Love"

We've all heard the phrase, "Do what you love and you'll never work a day in your life." This myth may lead people to pursue careers that match their interests without considering their other financial and lifestyle needs and values. After losing my banking job, I wondered if I'd have to choose between these two sets of priorities. But as my story shows, it's possible to balance both your career interests *and* your lifestyle needs – so long as you're open to creative ways of infusing what you love into your job.

Stefanie O'Connell, personal finance expert and author of *The Broke and Beautiful Life*, is another person in my field who has been able to achieve both her professional and financial goals by thinking outside the box. Growing up, O'Connell had always dreamed of performing on Broadway. So after graduating from New York University, she pursued her passion and pounded the pavement for several years. O'Connell eventually landed what seemed like a dream job performing in a multimillion-dollar musical playing at Madison Square Garden. The only problem? She was taking home just $1,600 a month in earnings. Anyone familiar with New York City real estate knows that rent money alone can eat away at that amount quickly.

"I was doing what I loved, but at the expense of a lot of other areas of my life," says O'Connell. "I gave up everything from basic financial security to once-in-a-lifetime celebrations with friends and family."

For O'Connell, the trade-off simply wasn't worth it in the end – but that didn't mean she was willing to settle for an unfulfilling job. Through her personal finance business, O'Connell still uses her public speaking skills by regularly presenting to companies and other groups. She also acts on the side.

"My current set-up allows me to create the financial stability I need, while also living the life I want," O'Connell explains. "Not only do I have the flexibility to perform on my own terms, but I'm finally able to make time for the other things I care about, like traveling and spending time with friends and family."

O'Connell's story demonstrates that you can love your career without working in your "dream job." In fact, you can often discover greater financial stability and overall happiness by opening yourself to alternative ways of fulfilling your interests.

"Work-Life Balance Is the Answer"

When people fail to achieve their goals by relying on the myths we've discussed, they might jump to the conclusion that work is always unpleasant and so their best option is simply to find a job that requires fewer hours, thereby allowing them to devote more time to their personal lives. I remember thinking this myself when I realized I couldn't make the lifestyle sacrifices required to build my own business full-time after my years in finance. But in fact, the concept of "work-life balance" – which suggests we should be evenly splitting our time between our professional and personal lives – is a myth in itself.

That's not to say that we should be working *more*. Employed Americans already spend an average of 52% of their waking hours either at work or getting to work[4] – a schedule that would stress out anyone. Even when we're not on the clock, many of us spend a lot of our free time obsessively checking and refreshing our work-related emails. As a result, jobs can easily invade and disrupt a good portion of our personal lives. It's no wonder that the American Institute of Stress says that work is "far and away the major source of stress for American adults."[5]

Yet even in today's overworked society, a less time-intensive job doesn't always make you happier. If you dislike your job, you'll still constantly be counting down to the weekend when you can live your "real life." And even when your "real life" finally does begin, you might be so drained that you choose mindless activities (read: binging on Netflix and cookies and cream ice cream) over more fruitful pursuits that actually align with your goals. I certainly know how hard it is to try to do anything productive, like hitting the gym or reading a book, after spending all day in a job I resent doing.

But don't just take my word for it. Jack Welch, former chairman and CEO of General Electric, is among the growing number of thought leaders who are speaking out against the concept of work-life balance. He explains, "There is no such thing as work-life balance. There are work-life choices, and you make them and they have consequences."[6] It's true – work and life are so fluid that striking a perfect balance is difficult, if not impossible. In fact, trying to do so may only make us more disappointed and frustrated.

So where does that leave the majority of us who want to work, without having our jobs encroach on the rest of our lives? The answer lies in finding the right job in the first place.

Lauren McGoodwin, founder of Career Contessa, a career advice site for women, has experienced firsthand the benefits of finding a good job. "When I found a well-fitting job, everything else just seemed to fall into place. I began to feel better physically, have more confidence, and my relationships got better as well – with my significant other and with myself. It's like the feeling you have after you endure a long, gloomy winter, and then walk out on that first sunny day of spring – you have that extra pep in your step. That's how I felt when things clicked into place with the right job."

Of course, finding the right job is easier said than done. Later in this book, we'll focus on helping you clearly define what a good job looks like for *you* instead of simply adopting the ideals that society at large (or even your well-meaning parents) might espouse. Based on the insights you gain, you can then take actionable steps toward making that job a reality.

Get in the Driver's Seat

We've all been fed subtle messages throughout our lives about what constitutes a good job. Some messages may be right, some may be sort of right, and others may be dead wrong. Now is a good time to revisit that past programming so that you can decide which messages correspond with your ideal life and which messages need to be discarded.

Block off 30 to 60 minutes on your calendar to think about which career myths you may have absorbed, consciously or subconsciously, and how they may have impacted your career. Grab a pen and paper to jot down notes and then find a quiet space (without your phone) to think through the following questions:

- Which of the career myths discussed have you been exposed to? Did you hear these myths from friends, family, co-workers, social media, or all of the above?
- Did one or more of these career myths influence your decision to work in your current job?
- Are some of these myths preventing you from changing jobs?
- Are some myths keeping you from considering certain professions or jobs?

I encourage you to reflect on your relationship to the career myths we've discussed, even if you consider yourself to be happy in your current job. Because once you understand your underlying motivations for choosing a particular path, you'll be able to get in the driver's seat and actively manage your career — whether that means staying the course or changing directions entirely.

Part II

Figure Out Your Starting Point

"You can't really know where you are going until you know where you have been."

– Maya Angelou

Based on the premise that your career and money choices are interdependent, let's shift our attention to the real reason you probably picked up this book: to come up with a plan for how to improve your career and finances, and gain some peace of mind in the process. In the coming chapters, you'll take the first step toward optimizing your situation by assessing where you stand now.

Because your career has such an overarching impact on your life, we'll start by putting your current job to the test. Specifically, we'll measure your role against five benchmarks of career satisfaction so that you can gain a clearer understanding of which aspects need improvement. You might also come away with criteria for what a fulfilling and enjoyable job looks like for you.

With a solid understanding of your current job situation, you'll then evaluate the financial resources you have to facilitate your ideal career path. First, I'll show you how to compile a report card that summarizes your financial health based on several key metrics, including your net worth, burn rate, financial runway, and credit score. You'll also be able to determine how much you're saving (if anything), and the minimum salary you need to fund your expenses.

Last but not least, you'll learn several effective and relatively painless ways to decrease your current living expenses (think pesky service fees, not your precious lattes), which can help you increase your savings rate and financial runway, while allowing you to expand your career choices (read: you could take a lower-paying but more satisfying job if you wanted).

So break out a pen and paper (or get access to helpful templates by visiting the website for this book at www.workyourmoneybook.com), grab a tasty snack, and let's get this party started!

Chapter 3
How's Your Job?

"How's it going?" is a phrase a lot of us probably hear and say at least 10 times a day. I remember greeting my banking colleagues with this line every Monday morning. Unsurprisingly, I didn't get a response most of the time: we all knew how it was going (read: not well), and besides, I had seen most of these people on Sunday working in the office, so I knew damn well how they were doing. Occasionally, someone would reply by saying, "Livin' the dream," but what they really meant was, "I'm living a baaad dream," or "I wish I got enough sleep to have dreams." A bunch of us would laugh in agreement, and then we'd go off to start our work.

During those years, I knew my situation was far from ideal – but beyond the long hours and lack of sleep, I had trouble pinpointing *why*. In a lot of ways, my role checked many of the boxes I had set for myself. I now realize that I had overlooked certain aspects of job satisfaction while overemphasizing others.

It turns out, job satisfaction can and should be evaluated on a number of levels. Whether you feel great, terrible, or blah about your job, it's helpful to figure out why you feel that way. And that's exactly what you'll be doing in this chapter.

Here's the plan. I'll walk you through five aspects of your job and provide questions for you to review in each area. You can use Table 3.1 at the end of the chapter to capture your responses (also available at www.workyourmoneybook.com) or simply make mental notes – whatever works best for you. If you'd like some sort of scoring system, think about whether each job area is 1) good, 2) okay, or 3) not so good. But know that not every area needs to be "good" across the board for you to be satisfied with your job. And the job areas you find most important today may change as you move through different phases of your life.

By the end of the chapter, you'll have a better sense not only of *how* it is going with your job, but also *why* it is going that way.

Job Factor 1: Are You Getting Value?

Translation: Do you like what you do on a day-to-day basis?

Have you ever met someone who claimed they figured out what they wanted to do for a living when they were very young (i.e., age 10 or younger)? You know, the person who says the one share of stock their parents bought for them was what got them interested in the stock market, and ever since then, they've wanted to work in mergers and acquisitions. I used to hear these stories and think, "Man, if only my parents bought me a share of stock when I was 10," or "Too bad I can't get paid for being good at Super Mario Kart." Now I think, "What the heck does a share of stock even have to do with mergers and acquisitions?!"

The reality is, many of us just fall into our first job after college. Our careers might be based on the companies that happened to recruit at our school, the one company that gave us an offer, or where we wanted to live. So the first job factor – the industry you work in and your day-to-day responsibilities – may or may not be exactly what you dreamt of, and that's okay.

Use the following questions to evaluate whether your industry and day-to-day job responsibilities align with your interests and skills.

Industry:
- Are you interested in the subject matter that your industry focuses on?
- Do you find yourself reading about developments in the industry in your free time, or could you care less?
- When your friends and family ask you about your job at social gatherings, are you excited to talk about what you do or do you quickly transition to a different topic?

Day-to-Day Responsibilities:
- Regardless of whether or not you're interested in your industry, does what you do on a day-to-day basis align well with your skills and interests?
- Do you find your work interesting, or are you assigned to work that no one else wants to do?
- Do you feel like you're learning something from your job and are challenged?
- Do you look forward to working with your clients?

Job Factor 2: Are You Adding Value?

Translation: Do you feel you're able to make an impact in your job?

All of us want to feel like we're adding value through our work. But alas, we're often blinded to the many ways in which we're making a positive difference in our jobs – an oversight that might cause us unnecessary dissatisfaction.

Dr. Amy Wrzesniewski of Yale University and Dr. Jane Dutton of the University of Michigan conducted a 2001 study on hospital janitors that highlights how our perception of our jobs can influence how we feel overall.[1] Some participants in the study said they viewed their job function as being limited to cleaning up after other people, and not surprisingly, this cohort seldom strayed from their predefined responsibilities. Others who worked in the same exact role described their job function as helping to create a positive experience for both patients and the organization itself. This group also saw their roles as more fluid and often took on additional responsibilities, interacted with other hospital staff and patients more, and generally viewed their jobs more positively. Same job, but two totally different perspectives. As the saying goes, sometimes perception is reality.

The truth is, you don't need to be the CEO of a company, saving lives, or ending world hunger to feel like you're making an impact in your job. You can benefit your organization simply by following through on assignments, keeping your manager on time for meetings, or cheering up your co-workers with entertaining memes. We *all* add value through our jobs, in one way or another – even if sometimes we have trouble seeing it.

On that note, I encourage you to consider the real and perceived impact you may be having at work by asking yourself the following questions:

- Do you feel what you do makes a difference in your team, organization, or industry? Have others, including your manager, co-workers, or clients acknowledged or recognized the impact you make?
- Do you think your work positively impacts other people outside of your business (e.g., your clients, broader society)?
- Do you find that you have the autonomy and freedom to make decisions at work?
- Do you have a clear understanding of your role, responsibilities, and performance expectations? Do you have clarity on how you could overdeliver in your role or make a bigger impact?
- Do you anticipate that your impact at work may grow in the near future (e.g., by taking on new projects or earning promotions)?

Job Factor 3: Are You Increasing Your Value in the Market?

Translation: Does your current role expand or decrease your future job options?

In middle school (i.e., grade 6 to 8), I remember you could gain street cred either by wearing the "in" name brand (whether it was Nike Air Jordans, Skidz plaid shorts, Levi's jeans, or anything from Abercrombie & Fitch), or by excelling at something, especially sports (playing piano, like me ... not so much).

Believe it or not, the ways you can increase your value in the job market – that is, opening up more options and opportunities for you in the future – aren't far off from these middle school tactics. You may be able to increase your marketability simply by being associated with certain name brands, whether it's paying your dues at Goldman Sachs or getting an MBA from Harvard Business School. You could also increase your market value by taking on a role that helps you build transferable skills and experiences, or by working in a field that is especially in demand (which, at the time of this writing, seems like engineering or anything that touches self-driving cars).

On the other hand, certain jobs can close doors quickly and limit your marketability, especially if you work in them for a long period of time. These may include jobs in declining industries, roles that are in the process of being automated, or job functions that build few transferable skills.

Take a look at your particular situation, and ask yourself the following questions to help determine if your current role opens or closes doors for you:

- Do you work for a prestigious or well-respected organization?
- Are you gaining skills that will make you marketable to a variety of employers and industries? Or does your job have a very narrow focus, meaning that in the future, you may only be able to transfer to a very similar organization or role?
- Think about former co-workers at your organization. What kinds of roles were they able to transition to (internally and/or externally)? Are those the kinds of roles you would be interested in as well?
- Do you envision wanting your boss's job one day? Does the leadership path at the organization inspire you?

Job Factor 4: Does Your Role Align with Your Values?

Translation: Do your office environment, work schedule flexibility, and employee benefits improve your overall quality of life?

Growing up, I'd describe my schedule and quality of life as quite regimented: waking up at 6 a.m.; going to school from 7 a.m. to 3 p.m.; attending soccer, cross country, or track practice until 5 p.m.; eating dinner at 6 p.m.; practicing piano at 7:30 p.m.; and doing homework for the rest of the night. And then repeat. The worst part was that I felt like I had no say in the matter; in fact, I downright hated some of these activities (especially homework). I assumed that the working world operated by the same oppressive and exacting rules as school, but that everything would be worth it someday as long as I was doing well professionally. Boy, was I dead wrong.

I know now that even if many aspects of your job are going well, you may not feel happy if it doesn't enable you to fulfill your interests and align with your priorities. So don't overlook or brush off the quality of life in your job, which includes company culture, work hours, employee benefits, how much you like the people, and office location and environment.

To gauge your quality of life in your job, ask yourself:

- Do you enjoy your physical office environment?
- Do you have a short commute (if that is something you value)?
- Do you like the people you're interfacing with on a day-to-day basis, such as your co-workers, clients, and/or vendors?
- Do you have someone at work you can confide in for personal and professional matters, such as celebrating good days, venting about bad days, and running questions by them that you may be hesitant to ask human resources (sometimes referred to as a work spouse)?
- Does your current job offer employee benefits that improve your quality of life, such as generous time-off policies (e.g., vacation days, sick days, family leave) and flexible work arrangements (e.g., ability to work from home, part-time work)? Are any important benefits missing that you wish you had?

- Does your current job allow you sufficient time to devote to your friends and family (if that's important to you)?
- Does your job allow you to participate freely in activities that interest you? For example, some companies limit employees' participation in any outside business activities (even small side hustles), or their ability to share ideas on a website or blog.

Job Factor 5: Do You Feel Valued?

Translation: Do you feel like you are being fairly rewarded through pay, promotions, and work responsibilities?

While people often give money and titles more weight than they should when evaluating their job satisfaction, these points are still important to consider. All of us want to feel like we're being properly acknowledged for our hard work both in financial and nonfinancial ways, not to mention that most people need some amount of income to be able to cover their living expenses and fund their financial goals.

Financial compensation includes your base salary, bonus, and stock payments. In some instances, compensation figures are publicly disclosed, like associate salaries at law firms. In other cases, you can often get a directional sense of whether you're being fairly compensated by checking salary-focused websites (e.g., salary.com and payscale.com), job review sites (e.g., glassdoor .com), and job listings for similar positions in your field. Conversations with recruiters could also help you gauge whether you're being paid fairly.

Compensation often goes hand in hand with your job level and promotions. Regardless of your role, you want to make sure that your responsibilities appropriately align with your job title or level. This matters because if you have less responsibility than others at a similar level, you may not be on a growth trajectory in your position. On the other hand, if you have more responsibility than others in your position, you may be being treated unfairly.

Ask yourself whether others in the same role at your or other organizations have similar backgrounds, experience, and responsibilities as you. You will also want to consider your opportunities for growth and advancement by comparing yourself to co-workers who have held similar titles at your organization. In particular, are you earning promotions: 1) at the same pace as others, 2) slower than others, or 3) faster than others? If you believe you are earning promotions slower than others at your level and with a similar performance history, think about what factors could be holding you back. These obstacles may include:

Your Manager

- Does your manager fully support your career development?
- Is your manager well-respected in the organization and progressing in his or her own career?
- Does your manager have the power and political capital to accelerate your career?

Exposure

- Are you being assigned to projects that allow you to gain the support of others in the organization, beyond your manager and immediate team?

Expectations/Feedback

- Do you feel like you have clear goals and expectations, or does your manager continue to move the finish line?
- Do you receive direct feedback from your manager throughout the year so you can improve and reach your career development goals, or do you receive mixed messages?
- If you receive an annual review, does the feedback surprise you or has it typically been communicated to you throughout the year by your manager?

From a nonfinancial perspective, compensation and recognition can be subtler. For example, feeling fairly treated and valued as a team member are signs of appreciation that you might seek at work. Your manager and co-workers could convey these messages by inviting you to important meetings, assigning you to more influential projects, seeking your perspective on work matters, or simply showing a personal interest in you rather than viewing you as just another cog in the machine.

Nonfinancial rewards can also be an important sign of your career trajectory, particularly in organizations with standardized salary amounts. For example, at top law firms (often known as "big law"), associates with the same tenure generally receive uniform base salary and bonus figures. When I asked my friend, who works at a big law firm, about this practice, he explained, "Sure, we all receive the same pay, but partners reward top performers with higher-profile or more interesting projects. Over time, this puts certain associates on track to become partners, while other lower-performing associates may eventually need to leave the firm."

Other forms of nonfinancial recognition may include invitations to participate in conferences and professional development trainings, as well as opportunities to gain more visibility at your company.

Summarizing Your Current Job Situation

While it would be amazing to find a job in which every job factor was positive across the board, that's probably not a realistic expectation, nor is it necessary for work satisfaction. For example, quality of life may not be as important to you right now because you're in your early 20s and single. Or maybe you're not super excited about the job content, but all the other job factors are good. Many people may also look outside of their careers to fulfill certain needs, rather than relying solely on their day jobs.

Lauren McGoodwin, founder of Career Contessa, says, "When I started thinking about what was important to me in a job, I realized it's sort of like budgeting your money – you're not going to be able to buy everything that you want, just like you're not going to get everything that you want in a job. When I came to that realization,

I was able to home in on what was most important to me in a company and a role."

Use Table 3.1 to create a snapshot of your current job situation (also available at www.workyourmoneybook.com). As a first step, you can jot down the ratings you may have assigned for each factor. Then, you'll prioritize each of the job factors, and finally, consider whether specific barriers stand in the way of improving the various aspects of your job situation.

Table 3.1   Evaluating Your Current Role.

Work Factor	Translation	Rating (good, okay, not so good)	Ranking, from Most to Least Important (1 is least important, 5 is most important)	Obstacles
1. Are You Getting Value?	Do you like what you do on a day-to-day basis?			
2. Are You Adding Value?	Do you feel you're able to make an impact in your job?			
3. Are You Increasing Your Value in the Market?	Does your current role expand or decrease your future job options?			
4. Does Your Role Align with Your Values?	Do your office environment, work schedule flexibility, and employee benefits improve your overall quality of life?			
5. Do You Feel Valued?	Do you feel like you are being fairly rewarded through pay, promotions, and work responsibilities?			

Now You Know

After completing the exercises and questions in this chapter, you should have a better understanding of what you like and dislike about your current role, as well as the obstacles that may stand in the way of improving your job situation. In Part 3, we'll build on these insights by helping you better understand what your ideal job looks like. You'll then be ready to learn about strategies for how to actually close the gap between the job you have and the job you want.

Chapter 4
Compiling Your Financial Report Card

"Is that everything?" I asked Claire during our first financial planning session together.
"I feel like I had an IRA ... or was that a Roth IRA?" she replied.
"I also remember contributing to a 401(k) three employers ago, but how would I go about tracking that money down?"

This type of exchange isn't unusual when I begin working with a new client. During our first session, I try to get a better understanding of the person's financial situation by having them aggregate their account balances in my client portal and upload backup documentation, such as account statements and tax returns. For some clients, this is a relatively straightforward exercise because they've been tracking their financial situation all along. However, for most people, like Claire, this may be the first time they've dug into their financial situation in so much detail.

As you can probably tell from my conversation with Claire, the initial onboarding process can be long and painful – but in the end, it pays off. I can tell that my clients come away feeling more in control of their financial situation, and ready to start making progress on their financial goals. In Claire's case, we were able to track down and consolidate several different retirement accounts that she had. Not only was Claire able to save a significant amount on investment fees, but she's gained peace of mind by being able to better track and manage her savings.

That's the power of compiling a financial report card – it can lay the groundwork for how you can improve your current situation to achieve your goals. Your financial report card will summarize where you stand financially based on four key metrics:

- **Net worth:** What you own minus what you owe
- **Burn rate:** What you spend, which influences what you save
- **Financial runway:** The number of months of living expenses you can cover with your current savings
- **Credit reports and scores:** Your history of borrowing money

In this chapter, I'll walk through each of the four key financial metrics while providing you with step-by-step instructions on how to create your financial report card. By the time you're done, you will have set the foundation for determining how to achieve many of your financial goals.

Metric 1: Net Worth

Translation: How much money do you have?

The first metric to figure out for your financial report card is your net worth. Your net worth is the difference between your total assets (i.e., what you own) and your total liabilities (i.e., what you owe) at some moment in time:

Net Worth = Assets (What You Own) – Liabilities (What You Owe)

Assets are anything of value, including money in your checking and savings accounts, investments in your 401(k) or a regular brokerage account, and the value of your home and car. Your two-year old futon would technically be considered an asset as well, but for

Table 4.1   Sample Completed Net Worth Template.

	01/01/20	02/01/20
Assets		
Checking and Savings	$15,000	$12,000
Retirement Savings (401(k), IRA)	$100,000	$105,000
Brokerage Account	$25,000	$27,000
(1) Total Assets	**$140,000**	**$144,000**
Liabilities		
Student Loan	$50,000	$49,000
(2) Total Liabilities	**$50,000**	**$49,000**
(3) Net Worth (1–2)	**$90,000**	**$95,000**

ease of calculating and updating your net worth, it's simplest to only include physical assets that are valued at $5,000 or more.

Liabilities are any money you owe to someone else, which include student loans, car loans, mortgages, and credit card debt.

Table 4.1 is an example of what a completed net worth statement looks like. The table is also available as a free resource on www.workyourmoneybook.com, in case you would like to use it when calculating your own net worth.

How to Calculate Your Net Worth

Step 1: Input Your Account Balances

Compile a list of all your accounts, including checking and savings accounts, retirement accounts, taxable brokerage accounts, and any loan accounts. You can then track down the balances of these accounts on an ongoing basis using either of the following techniques:

- **Old-School Method**: Manually check your balances at each account website or through account statements, and enter your balances into a spreadsheet. You can use the net worth template at www.workyourmoneybook.com as a guide to get started.

- **Automated Method**: Sync all of your financial accounts to a portal like mint.com or personalcapital.com. After signing up and syncing your accounts initially, these sites will automatically update your various account balances and calculate your resulting net worth – allowing you to quickly check your net worth at any time.

Why I Use the Old-School Method to Calculate My Net Worth

While the old-school method may seem inefficient, I actually prefer tracking my net worth this way because I find myself *more involved* in the process and *better aware* of any major changes.

Specifically, if I notice a big increase or drop in my net worth, I'm well positioned to dig deeper in that moment to figure out which accounts drove those changes. For example, I might realize I spent an unusually large amount of money in my checking account since my last net worth check-in. Perhaps there was a significant positive or negative change in the stock market that caused my net worth to shift. Or maybe I received my year-end bonus or annual 401(k) match from my company, which created a bump. Regardless of the situation, I feel more involved when entering the balances manually. I encourage you to try it out for yourself.

If you haven't tracked your net worth before, you may want to start by trying out both methods for a couple of months. At that point, you should be able to know which method works best for you.

Step 2: Input Your Home and Car Values

Regardless of the method you use, you will need to manually add the current market value for any homes and cars you own. Inputting these values may not be as clear-cut as inputting your account balances. Below, I try to simplify this exercise by providing a methodology for determining the estimated market values of cars and houses.

Car Values

Use the current market value rather than the price you paid, since the current market value is a better approximation of the price you would get today if you sold your car. Visit a site like edmunds.com or kbb.com to get an estimate of your car's current value. Since car values may not change in price from day to day or even month to month, you can update your car's value every 6 to 12 months in your net worth sheet, rather than on a more regular basis (i.e., you can use the same value for 6 to 12 months).

House Values

First, determine the current estimated value of your home. Websites like zillow.com and trulia.com can provide these price estimates while also allowing you to review recent sale prices of comparable homes. The value to use in your net worth sheet will depend on the relationship between the price you paid and the current estimated price.

- **Current Price ≤ Purchase Price**: Use current price for your house value.
- **Current Price > Purchase Price**: If the current price is greater than the purchase price, I suggest using the average of both figures instead of simply using the current estimated price. This helps to avoid artificially inflating your net worth if the estimated house values are wildly different than reality. In addition, in most instances, homes are more illiquid than other

financial assets (i.e., they take longer to sell), so the current estimated price may be much higher than what you are able to get when you sell. Lastly, this methodology helps you build in some cushion to factor in transaction costs (i.e., closing costs) and taxes that you may have to pay upon selling your home.

Similar to updating car values, you can update house values in your net worth sheet every six to 12 months unless there's a significant change in the market. If you have other physical assets in addition to your home and car that are worth at least $5,000, you might wish to add them to your net worth statement as well.

Breaking Down Liquid versus Illiquid Assets

I mentioned that houses are more illiquid than other financial assets. In general, liquidity refers to how quickly you can sell an asset for cash without impacting its market value. Assets that are more liquid can be bought and sold quickly at or near an asset's current price. Illiquid assets may take longer to sell to realize market prices, and if you need to sell an illiquid asset quickly, you may have to accept a discounted price.

For example, if a share of Apple stock were trading at $150 today, I know that I could likely sell a share of Apple for around that amount in short order – making it a liquid asset. On the other hand, if I wanted to sell a home with a current estimated market value of $500,000, I'd probably have to hire a real estate agent, who would create a listing and then hold open houses for a couple of weeks or months, before hopefully identifying a buyer willing to pay around that amount. Because real estate is typically difficult to sell quickly without accepting a significant cut in value, it is considered an illiquid asset.

Step 3: Rinse and Repeat

I recommend checking and compiling your net worth on a consistent schedule – that is, on or near the *same* day of each month, quarter, or year, so you can compare like results. I believe that checking once a month is ideal, because this frequency allows you to stay close to your finances and make any necessary changes in near real time. Personally, I have a one-hour recurring calendar event scheduled on the first day of each month to ensure I carve out time to update my net worth sheet.

Metric 2: Burn Rate

Translation: Where is your money going?

The next metric to tackle is your burn rate, or how much you spend during a set period of time. Burn rate matters because when you have a better understanding of where your money goes, you can assert more control over your finances. Even if you think you have an approximate sense of your burn rate, I strongly encourage you to complete the calculation as described in this section. Based on my experiences working with clients, I've found that most people's perceptions of their spending patterns differ drastically from reality (read: most people significantly underestimate how much they spend – I'm guilty of this as well!).

For example, my client Callie wanted to move to an apartment closer to her office, but thought that doing so would be impossible based on her monthly expenses. After calculating her burn rate, she was surprised to discover that approximately one-third of her monthly expenditures were going toward dining at restaurants. Callie now cooks a majority of her meals, which has helped reduce her spending and gotten her closer to her goal of living near work. That's the power of this burn rate exercise!

Table 4.2 Sample Completed Burn Rate Template.

	Monthly Cost	Annual Cost
Fixed Monthly Expenses	**$2,100**	**$25,200**
Rent	$2,000	$24,000
Internet	$100	$1,200
Variable Monthly Expenses	**$400**	**$4,800**
Groceries	$200	$2,400
Dining Out	$200	$2,400
Annual Expenses	**$275**	**$3,300**
Eyeglasses	$25	$300
Vacation	$250	$3,000
Total Burn Rate	**$2,775**	**$33,300**

How to Figure Out Your Burn Rate

My preferred method for figuring out your burn rate involves using a good ol' Excel spreadsheet and an automated financial portal that compiles financial information from across your accounts, such as mint.com or personalcapital.com. You can use the burn rate template at www.workyourmoneybook.com to get you started, or you can create your own (based on the example template in Table 4.2).

I recommend that you follow these best practices when creating your burn rate sheet so that you can gain valuable insights into your spending patterns without needing to do any additional digging.

- **Estimate Monthly and Annual Costs**: Create two columns to estimate each expense on a monthly and annual basis. This will help you see the annual amount you spend on monthly costs, as well as break down the implied monthly cost of annual expenses. You will also be able to compare your annual expenses to your annual net income, so that you can understand whether you have any extra savings available.
- **Bucket Expenses into Categories**: List expenses under three main categories:
  - **Fixed Monthly Expenses**: These include recurring expenses that don't change from month to month, such as housing

(rent or mortgage), non-mortgage debt (student loan), childcare and/or school, transportation (car, gas, tolls, public transportation), insurance (health, renters/homeowners), utilities (phone, cable, internet), and other fixed expenses (like a gym membership).

- **Variable Monthly Expenses**: These include expenses that occur every month, but may differ in amount, such as food (groceries, dining out, ordering in), entertainment (bars, concerts), beauty and personal care, dry cleaning, and shopping.
- **Annual Expenses**: These include expenses that may only occur once a year, such as vacations, certain insurance payments, repairs (home, auto), and professional fees (accountant, financial planner).

Getting the Data

You may know many of your fixed monthly costs, such as your rent or phone bill, right off the top of your head. Otherwise, you can look at your last bill, your latest credit card statement, or your financial portal of choice to track down those figures. For variable monthly expenses, you can estimate the average monthly amount you spend per category by reviewing your credit card statements or financial portal information over the last three or four months.

When filling out your fixed and variable monthly expenses in your burn rate sheet, simply:

- Complete the monthly cost column.
- In the annual cost column, multiply each of those monthly expenses by 12 to get the annual cost.

For annual expenses, you can take this reverse approach:

- Fill in these costs in the annual cost column.
- In the monthly cost column, divide each of the annual expenses by 12 to calculate the figure for the monthly column (while understanding that many of these expenses, such as vacations or emergency health costs, may not be monthly at all).

Are You Saving Any Money?

Now that you've calculated your annual burn rate, compare that figure to your annual net income to understand whether you are saving any money. You can determine your net income by using your last paycheck from the previous year or an online tax calculator.

To use your paycheck, look at your last paystub from the previous year. From your total gross income, subtract the taxes paid (e.g., federal, state, local, Social Security, Medicare). Alternatively, you could simply take your net income and add back any expenses you may have already tallied in your burn rate template, such as health insurance premiums and transportation costs, or any items that are not expenses, such as contributions to a 401(k) account.

For using an online tax calculator, input your gross income into an online tax calculator, such as the one offered by SmartAsset. The tool will estimate the federal, state, and local taxes you'll owe, and will output a net income amount.

Once you've pinpointed the relationship between your net income and living expenses, you can determine whether you're saving any money:

- **Net Income < Expenses**: You're not saving, likely racking up high-cost debt, and decreasing your net worth.
- **Net Income = Expenses**: You're not saving, simply breaking even, and neither adding to nor subtracting from your current net worth.
- **Net Income > Expenses**: You're saving and building your net worth.

Minimum Salary to Cover Burn Rate

In addition to being able to calculate how much you're currently saving, knowing your burn rate will allow you to determine the minimum salary you'll need to cover your living expenses. To calculate this, input various gross salaries into an online paycheck calculator to solve for the minimum income that will cover your annual burn rate.

Table 4.3   Your Current Financial Runway.

(1) Net Worth	
(2) Monthly Burn Rate	
(3) Months of Financial Runway (1 ÷ 2)	

Metric 3: Financial Runway

Translation: How many months of living expenses do you have saved?

You can now determine the months of financial runway you currently have by filling in your net worth and burn rate in Table 4.3 (also available at www.workyourmoneybook.com).

While using your net worth to calculate your financial runway will give you a sense of your overall runway, this method may include illiquid or not readily accessible assets, like equity in your home and savings in your retirement accounts. Both assets *do* contribute to your total financial runway, but in practice, you may not be able to tap either to facilitate a short-term transition.

As a result, it may also be helpful to calculate your liquid financial runway – instead of using your net worth in the calculation, use the total balance of any cash accounts and taxable brokerage accounts. As mentioned in Chapter 1, you should have at least three months of liquid financial runway saved in cash for an emergency fund. If you're a little low, don't worry – there are some ways to increase your financial runway, which we'll cover in the next chapter.

Metric 4: Credit Reports and Scores

Translation: How responsible have you been when borrowing money?

The last items to compile for your financial report card are your credit reports and credit scores, which are different, yet very much related.

A credit report provides detailed information about your credit history, including types of debt outstanding, loan balances, credit limits, account statuses, and payment history. Credit reports also include personal information about you, such as your social security number, date of birth, past addresses, and possibly, your employment history. These reports come from one of three US credit reporting agencies: Equifax, Experian, and TransUnion.

Companies and lenders use information in your credit report to calculate your credit score, which generally ranges from 300 to 850. Your credit score is then used by lenders to decide whether to allow you to borrow money, and if so, at what interest rate.

Taking a Closer Look at Credit Scores

Getting your credit score is pretty easy these days. Many banks and credit card companies provide credit scores to their customers for free, upon request. Some banks, like Chase and Discover, don't even require you to be a customer to receive a free credit score. And credit-focused sites, like creditkarma.com and creditsesame.com, offer free credit scores to anyone who creates an account.

If you've ever checked your credit score using multiple sources, you may have noticed differences in your score and wondered, what gives? Believe it or not, you actually have *multiple* credit scores that can differ based on a number of factors:[1]

- **Credit Information Used**: A credit score is typically based on a single credit reporting agency's report, rather than a combination of all three agency reports. And each credit reporting agency may have different information on file for you because lenders are not required to report account information to all three credit reporting agencies.[2] As a result, your credit score could vary based on which credit reporting agency provided the underlying information.
- **Methodology**: Your credit score could also differ based on the scoring model used to evaluate your credit information. While scoring models from Fair Isaac Corporation (FICO) and

VantageScore consider similar aspects of your credit file, they weigh the importance of each factor differently.

- **Timing**: The timing of your credit score calculation matters as well. Credit score providers do not calculate or update scores all at the same exact time, which may result in your various credit scores being based on different information.

Regardless of the type or source of your credit score, the scores can be valuable because they provide you with a directional sense of your credit strength.

Pro Tip for Getting Your Free Credit Scores

You can get a free credit score from a number of sources, but as noted, not all credit scores are created equal. As you reference your free credit scores, take note of the following:

1. **Type of Score**: The scoring model used to calculate the score. Most scores will be based on the FICO or VantageScore scoring models.
2. **Credit Reporting Agency Information Used**: Whether the score is based on information from Equifax, Experian, or TransUnion.
3. **Update Frequency**: If the score will be updated weekly, monthly, or another frequency.

Below are several places where you can get your free credit score, using the two most common types of scoring models:

FICO-Based Scores:

- **Discover**: You don't have to be a Discover customer to register for your free FICO score (based on your TransUnion credit report) through the company's website

(continued)

(continued)

(discover.com/free-credit-score/). Your score will be updated every 30 days.
- **Credit Cards**: Many credit card companies, such as American Express, Bank of America, and Chase, offer their customers free access to their FICO score.

VantageScore-Based Scores:
- **Credit Websites**: Credit-focused sites like Credit Karma and Credit Sesame offer free access to credit scores. Credit Karma provides scores from both Equifax and TransUnion, while Credit Sesame provides TransUnion credit scores. Both sites use calculations based on the VantageScore model.

How the FICO Scoring Model Works

One of the most widely used credit scoring models comes from FICO. Although FICO doesn't disclose the exact methodology it uses to arrive at your credit score, the company has provided guidance on how it weighs different factors.

Table 4.4 breaks down the factors FICO uses to determine your credit score, and the importance of each factor. We'll walk through each dimension so you can better understand what each factor means and how you may be able to improve that aspect of your credit file.

Payment History (Weight: 35%)

The biggest factor in determining your credit score is your payment history. Consistently paying the amount due on your loans

Table 4.4   FICO Scoring Methodology.[3]

Factor	Importance
Payment History	35%
Translation: Do you consistently pay the amount that is due on time?	
Tip: Use auto-pay for bills to ensure you stay on schedule.	
Credit Utilization	30%
Translation: How much of your available credit are you using?	
Tip: Use less than 30% of your available credit to score favorably on this factor.	
Length of Credit History	15%
Translation: How long have you been using credit?	
Tip: Keep your oldest credit cards open so you can demonstrate a longer credit history.	
New Credit	10%
Translation: Have you applied for a lot of new credit?	
Tip: Be thoughtful about applying for new credit cards, as this can count against you.	
Credit Mix	10%
Translation: Are you using a variety of credit types?	
Tip: While using a variety of credit is more favorable, this is often a tougher factor to control since it's based on personal needs.	

and credit cards on time could help improve your credit score, while not doing so may result in your credit score trending downward.

The lower your credit score, the less likely lenders will be willing to lend you money because there may be a higher chance they won't get all of their money back. And if lenders *do* end up lending you money, they may charge you higher interest rates.

This makes total sense. Picture two friends; let's call them Brad and Jordan. Both friends often ask you to borrow money for various reasons. Brad always remembers the amounts he borrows from you and promptly pays you back. Jordan, on the other hand, frequently forgets he even borrowed money from you, causing you to stress about if and when you should follow up with him, or if you should send him a passive-aggressive payment request via Venmo. Which friend are you more likely to lend money to in the future?

Credit Utilization (Weight: 30%)

Before jumping into what credit utilization is, let's clarify the main types of credit, which include installment loans and revolving credit. An installment loan, such as a mortgage or student loan, allows you to borrow a fixed amount of money, with required monthly payments based on a set schedule. For example, if you borrowed $400,000 via a 30-year fixed-rate mortgage at an interest rate of 4%, you would be required to pay $1,910 each month for 30 years. Revolving credit, on the other hand, allows you to borrow freely up to a set credit limit, and generally has required minimum monthly payments. Credit cards and home equity lines of credit are examples of revolving credit.

With that context, credit utilization, the second-largest factor in determining your credit score, is just a fancy term for describing the proportion of the total borrowing limit you're using on your revolving credit. Generally, the lower your credit utilization, the better your credit score. As an example, let's say across three credit cards you have a credit limit of $30,000. If you consistently have a balance of $15,000 outstanding across those cards, your credit utilization would be 50%, which is very high. Lenders like to see credit utilization below 30% for each account, and overall.

Length of Credit History (Weight: 15%)

The third-largest factor in determining your credit score is the length of your credit history, or the average age of your accounts. Lenders look more favorably upon borrowers with longer credit histories than those with short credit histories. This is one reason why people often seek advice on whether they should cancel a credit card that they no longer use or that carries a high annual fee. Although the answer may seem like an obvious yes, cancelling a credit card can negatively impact your credit score.

Should You Cancel That Credit Card You Don't Want?

When people ask whether they should cancel a credit card they don't want anymore, I tell them it depends on 1) their future borrowing plans, 2) the credit limit on the credit card, and 3) when they opened the card.

Future Borrowing Plans?

Are you planning to make a big purchase in the next year or two that will require a loan, whether that's a mortgage, auto loan, or student loan? If so, it could make sense to either hold on to that trusty credit card or, in the case of a card with an annual fee, convert it to a no-fee card to avoid a drop in your credit score. If you don't plan on seeking a loan within the next year, then canceling the card could make sense, but be sure to consider the other factors below before taking any action.

How Much?

Consider the credit limit of the card in question as well. When you cancel a credit card, you're decreasing the credit available to you, which will increase your credit utilization. If the credit limit on the card you want to cancel is low, then it won't have a huge impact on your overall credit utilization, but cancelling a card with a higher credit limit could materially increase your credit utilization and lower your credit score.

(continued)

(*continued*)

New or Old?

If the card you're cancelling is the newest card you've opened, then it's likely not contributing much to the age of your credit history, but if it is the oldest credit card you've had, then cancelling it could have some negative impact on your credit score. The impact may not be significant, however, depending on the rest of your credit profile.

Are you still fretting about whether or not to cancel that card? Don't. Credit scores are fluid, and will inevitably move up and down periodically. Even if you take some small action in the near term to decrease your credit score slightly, it likely won't have a long-term impact on your finances as long as you're consistently making on-time payments and keeping your credit utilization low.

New Credit and Credit Mix (Weight: 10% Each)

The last two factors, new credit and credit mix, each carry a 10% weight.

New credit refers to whether you've opened up a lot of new credit lines in a short period of time. FICO has found that having a lot of new credit makes you a greater risk to lenders.[4] So the next time you're trying to take advantage of a lucrative credit card sign-on bonus, be mindful that it could impact your credit score.

Credit mix looks at whether you're using both installment loans and revolving credit, or just one type of credit. While using both credit types is viewed as more favorable in the eyes of lenders, this is often a tougher factor to control since it's based on your personal needs.

Reviewing Your Credit Reports

It's important to review your credit reports periodically to ensure the information is accurate, and to confirm that no unauthorized accounts have been opened under your name. Luckily, you are entitled to one free credit report a year from each of the three credit reporting agencies. While you could request all three credit reports at the same time, I recommend you request one credit report at a time every four months. This method allows you to track your credit report throughout the year, rather than just once a year.

Pro Tip for Checking Credit Reports

Create a recurring calendar event to check your credit report every four months on the calendar app of your choice. This will increase the likelihood that you'll remember to request your credit report, actually make the time to review the reports, and ensure you'll have to use as little brain power as possible each time. Here is an example of how to put together the recurring calendar event:

Event Title: Request Free Credit Report

Location: annualcreditreport.com

Description: Jan 1: Equifax; May 1: Experian; Sept 1: Trans-Union

Summarizing Where You Are

Congratulations on compiling your financial report card! Now that you've completed this exercise, you have a far better sense of your financial situation than the vast majority of people.

Table 4.5   Financial Report Card.

Net Worth (Assets – Liabilities)	
Total Assets	
Total Liabilities	
Burn Rate (Annual Living Expenses)	
Monthly Burn Rate	
Monthly Savings (Annual Savings ÷ 12)	
Annual Savings (Net Income – Expenses)	
Minimum Salary to Cover Monthly Burn Rate (Use Online Paycheck Calculator to Estimate)	
Months of Financial Runway (Net Worth ÷ Monthly Burn Rate)	
Credit Reports and Score	
Credit Score and Type (i.e., FICO, VantageScore)	
Schedule for Requesting Free Credit Reports (Credit Reporting Agency, Month/Day to Request Report)	

I encourage you to use Table 4.5 (also available at www
.workyourmoneybook.com) to summarize your key findings. And
be sure to keep your financial report card close by because you'll
need to reference these figures periodically throughout the rest of
the book.

Chapter 5
How to Increase Your Financial Runway

Many people find investing to be the most interesting part of personal finance, and who can blame them? With numerous media publications devoted to covering every little movement in the stock market, and supposed investing experts yelling and screaming about stocks on cable television, it can be easy to think that not only is investing the *most interesting* part of personal finance, but the *most important* aspect as well.

But as we saw in Chapter 1, focusing on saving and keeping your expenses in check can significantly affect many aspects of your life. And believe it or not, saving money actually has a much bigger impact on your financial situation early on, compared to investing.

For illustration purposes, let's say you had annual living expenses of $100,000. In Table 5.1, you can see if you're able to save $10,000 a year, you've bought yourself a little over a month of financial runway. Assuming your investment portfolio could get an average return of 5%, your investments wouldn't generate $10,000 a year until you amassed a portfolio of at least $200,000 — not an immaterial sum of money to save up.

Table 5.1   Months of Financial Runway Added ($100,000 Living Expenses).

Savings Per Year	Investment Portfolio Required to Generate Savings Per Year (5% Return)	Months of Financial Runway Added
$500	$10,000	0.06
$5,000	$100,000	0.60
$10,000	**$200,000**	**1.20**
$20,000	$400,000	2.40
$30,000	$600,000	3.60
$40,000	$800,000	4.80
$50,000	$1,000,000	6.00

That's not to say investing isn't important. Investing is a key strategy that can help you reach your goals and live the life you want. That's why later on, we'll spend two chapters walking through the key investing concepts to know.

For now, though, let's focus on strategies you can use to increase your savings and financial runway, which will allow you to broaden the types of jobs you can take and free up more money to invest.

What Do You Love Spending Money On?

Before diving into which expenses to cut to increase your financial runway, think about the areas of your life you love to spend money on and which purchases bring you the most value. Ramit Sethi, author of *I Will Teach You to Be Rich*, calls these preferences your Money Dials. "Taking the time to identify your Money Dials can be powerful — it enables you to spend extravagantly on the things that truly matter to you, but also allows you to cut costs mercilessly on the things that don't matter." In addition to helping you be more deliberate with your spending, identifying what brings you value can help you begin to think about what financial goals you may want to set for yourself, and ultimately, the type of rich life you want to live.

I encourage you to take some time now to think about what areas you *love* to spend money on. Sethi has found that the three most common Money Dials are food, travel, and health and wellness. Personally, convenience is hands down my top Money Dial — I'm willing to spend money on products and services that improve my day-to-day quality of life, such as paying a premium for wireless earphones, spending a little extra to get products delivered to my doorstep instead of lugging them on the subway, and shelling out for a housekeeper rather than spending my Sunday afternoon doing laundry.

Your Financial Runway Action Plan

Now that you have some perspective on what you love to spend money on, let's take a closer look at some ways you can decrease spending on the things you don't love as much. Table 5.2

Table 5.2   Strategies to Decrease Expenses.

	Low Impact	Medium Impact	High Impact
Low Effort	• Eliminate unnessary bank and credit card fees.	• Cancel unnecessary subscriptions. • Negotiate cable, internet, and phone fees.	
Medium Effort		• Save on shopping expenses. • Maximize credit card rewards. • Decrease food costs.	
High Effort			• Cut housing expenses. • Minimize taxes. • Reduce credit card and student loan debt.

summarizes the strategies we'll be covering for increasing your financial runway.

The suggestions vary based on the amount of effort needed from you, as well as the potential impact to your burn rate. The strategies that are easiest to implement may have the smallest impact, such as decreasing ATM fees, but you may be able to take action on these right away (because who the heck loves paying ATM fees?).

On the other hand, the areas that could have the largest impact — such as decreasing your housing costs — may require you to think through your preferences and research alternatives, which could take months. For now, you may simply want to understand and bookmark these more time-intensive strategies and then continue reading the book. You can always return to this chapter later, once you've had time to think through all of your goals and priorities — at which point, you may be able to be more decisive about which strategies to use to develop a workable financial plan.

Cut Low-Hanging Fruit

Level of Effort: Low

Let's start off with the easy stuff; this includes eliminating small bank or credit card fees you may be incurring without even realizing it, cancelling ongoing services and subscriptions that you no longer use, and negotiating existing cable, internet, and phone plans. While the monetary impact of cutting these expenses will be low to medium, you can take action on them pretty quickly.

Eliminate Bank and Credit Card Fees

Impact: Low

A lot of the fees that banks and credit cards charge are completely avoidable. Table 5.3 highlights the strategies I recommend for decreasing or eliminating these fees.

Table 5.3   How to Eliminate Bank and Credit Card Fees.

Type of Fee	What It Is	How to Avoid This Fee
1. ATM Fee	A bank may charge you ATM fees when you withdraw money from an ATM that is outside of your bank network. Typically, your bank will charge you a fee, and the bank that owns the ATM you're using will charge a separate fee.	Switch to a bank that has more conveniently located ATMs, or switch to a checking account that charges no ATM fees, such as the Schwab High Yield Checking Account.
2. Foreign Transaction Fee	Your bank may charge you foreign transaction fees that generally range from 1% to 3% for using your credit or debit card outside of your home country. When using debit cards to withdraw money from a foreign ATM, you may have to pay ATM fees *and* foreign transaction fees. On a $100 withdrawal, you could end up with only $90 after all those fees!	Use credit and debit cards that do not charge foreign transaction fees when traveling abroad. A quick online search will help you identify cards that may work for you.
3. Monthly Service Fee	Some bank accounts charge monthly service fees if you don't maintain a certain amount of money in your checking or savings account.	Maintain the minimum amount of money required in the account so you don't incur the fee, switch to a lower-tier account, or switch banks entirely to one that won't impose minimum balance requirements on a particular account.
4. Late Payment Fee	You may incur fees from your bank as a result of paying your credit card bill late.	Set your credit card payments to auto-pay, but make sure to review each monthly statement for fraudulent transactions.

Cancel Unnecessary Subscriptions

Impact: Medium

Many companies now use an ongoing subscription model when charging for their products or services. While each subscription may only cost $10 to $15 a month, the total costs can really add up. In fact, I've been able to help some clients save hundreds of dollars a month simply by identifying and reminding them to cancel unused subscriptions. I recommend that you review your existing subscriptions at least once a year and ask yourself the following questions:

- Do I still use this service?
- Do I have other services that serve the same purpose?
- Are multiple people in my family using this service? If so, could I combine our subscriptions under a family plan that may allow all of us to save money?

Negotiate Cable, Internet, and Phone Fees

Impact: Medium

Many people have found success in lowering their monthly fees for cable, internet, and phone service by calling providers and requesting a lower rate, or by saying they are considering cancelling the service and switching to a new provider. If a provider is unwilling to lower your monthly fee, you could instead try to request some type of service upgrade at no cost, such as a premium channel, faster internet speed, or a larger phone data plan. While these extras won't increase your financial runway, they could still improve the quality of your life (because being able to watch *Big Little Lies* is cool, but being able to watch it for free is even cooler).

I recommend you take 10 to 20 minutes to review your account statements for any bank and credit card fees you're incurring, as well as any unused subscription fees you are paying. Use the strategies we've discussed to come up with a plan for eliminating or decreasing these fees. Then, carve out another 20 to 30 minutes to call your cable, internet, and phone providers to try to score a lower monthly rate or extra perks that you may value. You might be surprised by how much additional money you'll be able to save by decreasing these costs.

Expend Some Effort

Level of Effort: Medium

The strategies discussed in this section — like decreasing your shopping, travel, and food costs — might take a little more energy, but they should not be particularly controversial.

Save on Shopping Expenses

Impact: Medium

Table 5.4 highlights two ways to save on shopping, including 1) enrolling in free loyalty programs and 2) using cash-back shopping for online purchases.

Table 5.4   Shopping Strategies to Save Money.

Strategy	Loyalty Programs	Cash-Back Shopping
1. Benefits	You can save money at eligible stores seamlessly after signing up.	You'll be able to save money on nearly everything you purchase online by adding one small step to your shopping journey.
2. How It Works	1. Sign up for a loyalty program and sync your credit and/or debit cards. 2. You'll earn cash back anytime you spend money at a participating store.	1. Sign up for a cash-back portal. 2. Every time you make an online purchase, go to your cash-back portal first, instead of going directly to the online store. 3. Search for the store you want to shop at and click through to the online store via the portal link. 4. Make a purchase as you normally would, and you're off to earning 1% to 30% cash back per transaction.
3. Example Services	Drop	Rakuten, Mr. Rebates

Maximize Credit Card Rewards

Impact: Medium

Credit card points are another easy way to receive cash back, save on everyday purchases, or save on your next vacation. These days, most credit cards offer cardholders some type of reward for using their cards. However, not all credit card rewards programs are created equal — some credit cards offer the same cash-back or credit card rewards percentage no matter what you buy, while other credit card rewards programs offer increased rewards for certain spending categories, such as food and travel.

To determine the best credit card for you, set aside 30 minutes to review your spending patterns from the past year. If your spending is concentrated in a couple of categories, search for a credit card that allows you to earn more points per dollar spent in those categories. If your spending is evenly distributed across categories, it could make sense to look for a card that provides solid credit card rewards for all types of spending rather than increased rewards for certain categories.

Decrease Food Costs

Impact: Medium

While everyone needs to spend a certain amount on food, you might be overindexing in this category, particularly if you rely on food delivery services or go to restaurants frequently. Even when people buy groceries to try to save money and eat healthier, they may end up overspending (like when spontaneous social plans come up midweek that cause the groceries you bought last Sunday to go bad).

Take some time to review how much you spend on food overall, as well as the breakdown between restaurants and groceries. Determine your average costs when you dine in and get delivery, and then identify if there are ways to decrease those costs. For grocery spending, think back to your behavior over the last month, including:

- How often did I cook?
- Did certain barriers keep me from cooking?

- Did a lot of my groceries go bad before I could use them?
- What strategies could I use to decrease waste?

How My Wife and I Decreased Food Costs

My wife and I reached a point several years ago when we realized we should be more deliberate about our food costs. At the time, we were frequently ordering in from or dining at restaurants in all price tiers — from the Chipotle down the street to three-Michelin-starred restaurants. However, we had both begun to notice a pattern of extreme dissatisfaction with restaurants in the middle price range that were more expensive than a fast food joint, but not as expensive as a high-end establishment. The food was never memorable, yet the meal would still set us back a fair amount; in fact, if we had a couple rounds of drinks, the bill could easily add up to $100 for two people.

The solution we came up with was to replace our moderately priced restaurant purchases with home-cooked meals. We ended up spending less money than if we had gone to a mediocre restaurant, and the food often tasted much better (if I do say so myself). Best of all, because we had saved some money, we didn't feel bad the next time we splurged on a high-end restaurant.

Tackle the Hard Stuff

Level of Effort: High

While cutting smaller costs may be easiest, reviewing and decreasing your largest costs, such as housing, taxes, and credit card and student loan debt, could make the biggest impact on your financial runway. For example, if you decided to stop your $5-a-day latte fix, that'd only save you $1,825 a year. And think of the consequences!

Without your daily dose of caffeine, you may find yourself more irritable, less productive, potentially snoozing in dirty subway cars or at your office, and eventually, living in a van down by the river. On the other hand, if you're able to lower your monthly rent from $2,500 to $2,200, you'll save $3,600 a year — nearly double the latte strategy, and probably a much less painful route.

Cut Housing Expenses

Impact: High

Housing is by far the largest expense in most people's budgets, making up 33% of the average American's total expenses, according to the Bureau of Labor Statistics.[1] In terms of what it "should" be, financial planners recommend you limit your housing expenses to a *maximum* of 28% of your annual gross income (28% is an upper limit, not the target goal). If you make an annual salary of $100,000, you should be aiming to spend no more than $2,333 a month on housing, or $28,000 a year. Of course, the less money you divert to housing costs, the more you'll have available to fund other financial goals, including being able to shore up your financial runway.

If you're currently well beyond the 28% threshold, don't worry. Here are some ways you may be able to decrease your housing expenses and fuel more financial runway:

- **Negotiate Your Rent**: If you've been a good tenant (i.e., consistently pay rent on time, adhere to building rules, do not damage property), your landlord may be open to lowering your rent if you ask. If your landlord balks at lowering your rent, you could request other value-add amenities instead, such as free access to the fitness center or discounted or free parking.
- **Refinance Your Mortgage**: If you own your home, explore if refinancing your mortgage could decrease your monthly payment. Be sure to take into consideration the closing costs involved and how much longer you'll stay in the home to determine whether any monthly savings would offset the upfront costs.

- **Align Your Space and Amenities with What You Value**: Determine the amount of space and type of amenities you want and match those preferences to your living situation. For example, if you're living in a new high-rise building with a lot of amenities that you don't value or a big house with a chef's kitchen you don't use, you could save money by moving to a place that better matches your needs. Not only will you be able to decrease your monthly housing payment, but you may also be able to lower other housing expenses, such as utilities, cleaning fees, and furniture costs.
- **Evaluate Where You Live**: Housing prices will usually be higher for units that are perceived as more desirable because they're in a supposedly "better" location. If you're paying high housing prices because you live within close proximity to community amenities that you don't take advantage of — such as top-rated schools, a lively nightlife district, or public transportation — it could make sense to relocate to a less expensive area within the same city.
- **Get a Roommate**: Adding a roommate could help you live in a nicer area or building, while enabling you to pay less than if you lived on your own.

Your home can have a significant impact on your daily happiness and comfort, as well as the amount of money you're able to save each month. As you evaluate your housing situation, be sure you understand your preferences and priorities, and take *all* factors into consideration when determining whether a change makes sense for you.

Minimize Taxes

Impact: High

Nobody likes paying taxes, and most people want to minimize the amount of taxes they have to pay (within the law). Luckily, there are surprisingly easy ways to cut your tax bill that could help you save a significant amount of money.

Reduce Taxes Through Employee Benefits

You may be able to save a fair amount on your tax bill just by taking full advantage of your employee benefits. Regardless of whether you're funding a retirement, health care, or commuter account, the general mechanics are the same:

- You decide to contribute some portion of your salary to an account to fund your retirement, health care expenses, and/or transportation costs.
- Those contributions decrease the amount of your income that is subject to federal taxes in the year of contribution. With a lower taxable income amount, you'll generally owe less in taxes.

For example, say that you make $100,000 a year. You decide to contribute $2,000 to your health savings account this year. Instead of your taxable income equaling $100,000, just $98,000 would be subject to taxes.

Table 5.5 outlines some employee benefits you can use to save on your current-year tax bill.

Other Tax-Saving Strategies

Table 5.6 highlights strategies outside of your employee benefits that could help you save on taxes, including by contributing to a 529 plan, making charitable donations, or deducting mortgage interest and property taxes for home ownership. Keep in mind that some of these strategies require you to itemize deductions on your federal tax return to benefit from tax savings.

What the heck does itemizing deductions actually mean? When you file your federal tax return each year, you are allowed to subtract a standard or itemized deduction from your income to arrive at the amount of your income that is subject to tax. You'll generally choose the higher amount between the standard and itemized deduction, which will minimize your taxes. The standard deduction is a fixed amount based on your filing status, age, vision status, and whether someone else can claim you as a dependent. Itemized deductions are

Table 5.5 Employee Benefit Tax-Saving Strategies.

Employee Benefit	Purpose of Savings	Tax Benefits	Considerations
401(k) Plan	Retirement	Pretax contributions result in a decrease in your current-year taxable income.	Withdrawals of pretax contributions from your 401(k) will be taxed as income.
Flexible Spending Account	Health Care	Contributions decrease your current year taxable income.	These are typically "use it or lose it" accounts, so most contributions must be used in the same year of contribution. Some companies may give employees an additional 2.5-month grace period to spend monies or allow you to carry over up to $500 in unused monies.
Health Savings Account	Health Care	Contributions decrease your current year taxable income.	You must be on a high-deductible health plan to get access to a health savings account.
Commuter Benefits	Transportation	Pretax contributions decrease your current year taxable income.	Pretax contribution limits for transit and parking may be lower than your monthly transportation costs.

based on eligible expenses that you incurred throughout the year, like mortgage interest; state, local, and property taxes up to $10,000; and charitable deductions. For 2019, the standard deduction for single filers was $12,200.[2] As a single filer, if the amount of your eligible expenses to itemize is less than $12,200, then you would take the standard deduction.

Table 5.6   Other Tax-Saving Strategies.

Strategy	Purpose of Savings	Tax Benefits	Considerations
529 Plan	Education	Some states provide a state tax benefit for contributing to a 529 plan in the state where you live, while others give you a benefit for contributing to any 529 plan.	Not all states provide a state tax benefit, and generally, proceeds must be used for qualified educational expenses, or withdrawals could be subject to federal, state, and local taxes, as well as penalties.
Mortgage Interest	Housing	Mortgage interest increases the amount of itemized deductions you have for the tax year, which could decrease your tax liability if you itemize deductions.	Only interest up to $750,000 in mortgage debt can be claimed. You must itemize deductions.
Property Taxes	Housing	Property taxes increase the amount of itemized deductions you have for the tax year, which could decrease your tax liability if you itemize deductions.	You are limited to deducting a combined maximum of $10,000 per year across property taxes, and state and local taxes. You must itemize deductions.

Reduce Credit Card and Student Loan Debt

Impact: High

Decreasing the expense of your debt could take time, but it has the potential to significantly reduce your burn rate, particularly if you are able to eliminate high-cost credit card debt.

Table 5.7   Debt Inventory.

Lender	Type of Debt	Outstanding Balance	Interest Rate

The first step in cutting down your debt is to list out all of the debt that you have. Use Table 5.7 (also available at www .workyourmoneybook.com) or your own template to create an inventory of your outstanding debt, including:

- Lender
- Type of debt
- Outstanding balance
- Interest rate

You may have already compiled some of this information in Chapter 4 when you came up with your net worth and burn rate, so be sure to reference that work before duplicating efforts.

For student loans, specify under type of debt whether the loan is a federal or private student loan. You can figure this out by looking at the latest statement from your student loan provider, or in the case of federal student loans, verifying your outstanding loans through the National Student Loan Data System (nslds.ed.gov).

Determine Options to Decrease Debt Cost

There are three main ways to decrease your debt cost or simplify your debt repayment for credit cards and student loans:

1. **Request an Interest Rate Reduction (Credit Cards Only):** Receive a lower interest rate on your existing debt.
2. **Consolidate (Federal Student Loans Only):** Combine multiple federal student loans together into one loan; does not decrease the weighted average interest rate on your debt.

3. **Refinance (Credit Cards and Student Loans):** Could be used to combine multiple loans together into one loan, potentially decrease the interest rates on your debt, and/or give you better terms on your new loan.

Request an Interest Rate Reduction (Credit Cards Only)

While student loan providers typically don't negotiate interest rates, your credit card issuer may be open to exploring this option.

Before making a call to request a rate reduction, be sure to arm yourself with some relevant information, including your current interest rate, the interest rate on comparable credit cards, and your credit history and credit score (which you should have from Chapter 4).

Once on the call, if the initial customer service representative you talk to lacks the authority to make such a decision, ask to speak to their supervisor. Regardless of who you speak to, try to remain calm, collected, and patient during your discussion — after all, the biggest (and only) downside is that you'll end up with the same interest rate that you have currently. That being said, CreditCards .com research found that three out of four cardholders who ask for a lower interest rate get it![3] (How's that for motivation?)

Consolidate (Federal Student Loans Only)

Debt consolidation offers you the opportunity to combine your outstanding federal student loans into one loan. (Private student loans aren't eligible to be consolidated under the Federal Direct Loan Program.) Consolidation could be a great way to help you more easily track and pay your loans; however, it will not lower your interest rates. The interest rate of your new consolidated loan will simply be the weighted average of the interest rates of your outstanding federal student loans.

Nonetheless, consolidation *could* decrease your monthly loan payment, because combining several small balance loans may qualify you to extend the length of your new loan from the standard

10-year term to as long as a 30-year repayment period.[4] Be aware that while your monthly loan payment might decrease in such cases, the total amount of interest paid for the life of the loan would increase because you'd be paying the loan over a longer period of time, unless you decide to prepay your loan.

Refinance (Credit Cards and Student Loans)

Refinancing involves replacing your existing loan(s) or credit card balances with a new loan or credit card that (hopefully) provides better terms. The main ways to refinance credit card debt are through balance transfers or a personal loan. For student loans, you could refinance federal and private student loans through a new private student loan.

Credit Cards

- **Balance Transfers**: Transferring your existing credit card balances to a new card that offers an introductory 0% interest rate for 6 to 18 months could provide you with some temporary relief from interest accruing. Your goal would be to create a plan to pay off the new credit card balance entirely before the introductory 0% interest rate period ends. When deciding whether to open a balance transfer card, be sure to evaluate the introductory interest rate offered (hopefully 0%), how long the introductory rate will be applicable, the balance transfer fees, and how much can be transferred to the new card. A balance transfer card could be an attractive move if the interest savings outweigh any fees, and if the introductory 0% interest rate period gives you enough time to pay off your credit card debt in full.
- **Personal Loans**: Refinancing through personal loans is an alternative strategy for reducing credit card debt. Personal loans often have upfront fees associated with them, so you'll need to consider the all-in-fees you'll be paying to see if refinancing your existing credit card debt would be financially beneficial.

Student Loans

- **Private Student Loan Refinancing**: Refinancing through a private student loan lender allows you to combine all of your various student loans (federal and private) into one loan payment. Unlike a federal consolidation loan, for which the interest rate is simply the weighted average interest rate of your existing loans, the interest rate for your new refinanced student loan will be based on your particular financial profile, including your credit score, current asset and liability profile, and debt-to-income ratio or free cash flow (typically, your net income less any debt and housing payments). If you have a strong financial position, you may be able to score a lower interest rate by refinancing. In addition, most lenders do not charge a fee to refinance your student loans.

How to Think About What to Do with Your Student Loans

It can be overwhelming to figure out which options to look into, particularly for your student loans. Veena Ramaswamy, Vice President of Strategy at student lender CommonBond, recommends first determining if you may be eligible for the Public Loan Service Forgiveness program. "For those not eligible, look into whether refinancing could help you achieve your goals, whether it be cost savings via lower monthly payments or paying off your loans faster, and if refinancing isn't an option, consider whether consolidation would simplify your situation or help improve your cash flow."

Your New and Improved Financial Runway

Now that you've had a chance to eliminate or decrease some of your current expenses, you are ready to uncover your new and improved financial runway! Go back to your earlier work in this

Table 5.8   Your Updated Financial Runway.

(1) Net Worth (from Chapter 4)	
(2) Monthly Burn Rate (update based on work in this chapter)	
(3) Months of Financial Runway (Net worth ÷ Monthly burn rate)	
(4) Minimum Salary to Cover Monthly Burn Rate (use online paycheck calculator to estimate)	

chapter and estimate how much in monthly expenses you were able to cut. Next, input your new and improved monthly burn rate in Table 5.8 (available at www.workyourmoneybook.com as well). You should then be able to recalculate your financial runway and minimum required salary. Your updated minimum salary will be an important threshold to keep in mind as we delve deeper into what jobs may be a good fit — both professionally and financially.

Lastly, if you were able to take advantage of some of the debt-saving strategies, it may be helpful to update your original loan inventory for any interest rate, balance, and monthly payment changes. For balance transfers specifically, make sure to note in your loan inventory and online calendar app when the 0% interest rate period expires.

Part III

Optimize Your Job

"So I was sitting in my cubicle today, and I realized, ever since I started working, every single day of my life has been worse than the day before it. So that means that every single day that you see me, that's on the worst day of my life."

– *Peter Gibbons*, Office Space

Now that you have a clear grasp of both your professional and financial situations, you're primed and ready to explore strategies for improving your job satisfaction.

The key to making the right career choices is self-knowledge. That's why this section starts by helping you picture your ideal role. You'll then build on the work you did in prior chapters to identify how your current and target roles may differ. Depending on the extent of the discrepancies and your financial needs, you can then determine which strategy or strategies would be most effective to help you find greater fulfillment in your career.

The remainder of this section will walk through three ways to improve your job situation, including by tweaking, supplementing, or replacing your current role. Job tweaks enable you to better align your current role with the career priorities you'll be identifying. Supplementing your job allows you to test how it feels to wear a different hat, while also helping fill the gaps that may exist between your current and ideal jobs. Switching jobs altogether is of course the most drastic (and in some cases, financially risky) approach of all, so we will be devoting two chapters to this strategy.

By the time you've finished reading this section, you should have a clear concept of your desired career path *and* a game plan for how to achieve it. Be sure to go to www.workyourmoneybook.com to access helpful templates that you can use for the various exercises in this section.

Chapter 6

What Does a "Good" Job Look Like for You?

"What about a start-up or venture capital?" my friend suggested.
"I don't know – aren't those super hard to get into, especially venture
capital, and aren't start-ups pretty risky?" I responded.

I had asked my friend to help brainstorm other industries for me to transition to, but it didn't seem like we were making much progress. I knew my job at the time wasn't the right fit, but it seemed like we were just guessing at what could be good career paths based on what sounded "cool" or "sexy." Instead of relying on gut feeling or what other people said was a "good" job, which is how I ended up in investment banking in the first place, I wanted to be able to have a structured way to think about this decision, preferably with concrete data to help guide me.

Finding the right job might sound relatively straightforward, but it's not. It's actually a complicated problem, with a lot of different factors to take into account and balance. I realized that breaking the process into bite-sized tasks would make it much more manageable. As a first step, I decided to analyze what a good role looked like for me by reflecting on the two full-time positions I had held, as well as my summer internships, high school jobs, big class projects, and extracurricular activities. This was my way of beginning to gather some real data points.

For the remainder of the chapter, I'll walk you through several exercises that will help you get more clarity on your interests, strengths, preferences, and priorities. In particular, the exercises will focus on helping you understand what you like, what you don't like, what you're good at, and what you may want life to look like moving forward. After completing this chapter, you should be better positioned to align what you want with potential industries and jobs.

Part 1: Interests and Strengths

The exercises in Part 1 will help you identify your interests and strengths by reviewing your past experiences, looking at your outside interests, seeking feedback from others, and taking personality assessments.

Exercise 1: What You Like

(30–60 Minutes)

It may sound odd to have to go through an exercise to identify your preferences. Most of the time, you just *know* what you like. Take food, for example – I know I love pizza, burgers, Peking duck, and foie gras (damn it, why can't I be one of those people that likes vegetables or more healthy foods?!). When it comes to working out, I love going on a nice long run and doing push-ups, but I really don't like doing pull-ups.

With work, what we like gets a lot murkier. We often find ourselves struggling to reconcile a number of conflicting external influences. There are our parents, who understandably want their children to be able to support themselves by earning reliable incomes, which impacts the ideas and values they impart. Then there are the messages we hear on TV and in movies, which often glamorize less stable career paths. And then, of course, our peers may be influencing us with their own beliefs about money and careers. No wonder it can be tough to know whether you *really* like a job, on your own accord. That's why you'll be going through some exercises to help you cut through all that noise, so you can confirm what you genuinely like.

Either on a piece of paper or using your favorite computer tool (e.g., Word, Excel), list all of the jobs you've had since high school, and the approximate dates you held each job. If you've had hobbies, class projects, or other extracurricular activities that took up a meaningful amount of time, put those on your list as well. Under each role, write a couple of sentences about what you liked about the job or role and what you didn't like so much. Try to be as specific as possible about the good and bad aspects.

Some factors that could help jumpstart your brainstorming include:

- **Schedule**: Flexible or rigid
- **Work Hours**: Not much, average, or a lot
- **Predictability**: Proactive or reactive
- **Stress Level**: Low, medium, or high
- **How You Were Managed**: Micromanaged or full autonomy
- **Managing**: Individual contributor or manager
- **Work with Others**: Independent or team-based work

My Examples of What Was Good and Wasn't Good

Here are some examples based on the early jobs I had:

Company/Activity: Giant Eagle

Role/Title: Grocery Bagger
Dates: June 1999–August 1999

(continued)

(continued)

What Was Good: Giant Eagle was a new grocery store that was clean and had good lighting. It was a relatively pleasant place to go to work for a first job. Many of the employees were my age, so we would often talk while working and several of those employees became my friends. Having people to interact with during the work day made the time pass much faster and made going to work more enjoyable.

What Wasn't Good: Giant Eagle paid me minimum wage ($5.15/hour back then). I was often assigned to retrieve shopping carts from the parking lot in 90-degree temperatures while wearing a long-sleeve dress shirt and dress pants (the mandatory dress code). Shifts required me to stand for two to three hours at a time. While my co-workers helped me pass the time, my actual job was quite repetitive and boring.

Company/Activity: Shop 'n Save

Role/Title: Cashier

Dates: March 2000–May 2000

What Was Good: I was earning more than my role at Giant Eagle ($0.35 more per hour).

What Wasn't Good: Shop 'n Save was a much older grocery store; it seemed dirty and depressing, so it wasn't a particularly good work environment. Many of my co-workers were older and seemed unhappy. As a result, we didn't talk to one another much, which made my work shifts feel longer than when I worked at Giant Eagle.

Company/Activity: Wachovia

Role/Title: Analyst, Derivatives Sales

Dates: June 2005–May 2006

What Was Good: I had a very supportive manager, so even though I was fresh out of college, I was given a lot of responsibility and was assigned interesting projects and deals. I also had the opportunity to get involved in activities outside of my day-to-day job, including recruiting new analysts. Through my involvement with recruiting, I was able to build a compelling business case for why Wachovia should recruit analysts from my alma mater. Developing that recruiting initiative from idea to execution helped me feel empowered.

What Wasn't Good: I have always valued being part of a diverse population reflecting different races, ethnicities, and backgrounds. However, Wachovia was based in Charlotte, North Carolina, where the population was fairly homogenous (at that time). While Charlotte is a great city for families, it didn't provide many social opportunities for recent graduates beyond the same four bars and restaurants. I also typically worked 11-hour days, starting at 7 a.m. This was particularly challenging because I like to have some time for myself before heading to work. Sitting on the trading floor and fielding calls from clients all day brought a very reactive dimension to the role that I disliked.

Exercise 2: What You're Good At

(30–60 Minutes)

"What is your competitive advantage?" asked Aaron.

My friend wasn't trying to be brash. His question came up as part of an informal coffee chat I had set up when I was thinking about changing industries from investment banking. I wanted to meet with Aaron, who had worked in private equity for several years, to learn more about the industry and find out if my background would be an attractive fit.

During our conversation, Aaron was trying to better understand what unique skills I had that would motivate him or a recruiter to choose me for a position over someone who had the *exact* background the company was seeking. While I wasn't able to dazzle Aaron with my non-answer, his questioning did make me realize I needed to be able to answer this question not only for interviews, but for myself as well.

To figure out how you're smarter, faster, or better, you'll first have to identify what you're good at. Refer back to the list of jobs, hobbies, class projects, and other extracurricular activities you developed in Exercise 1 and then add two rows below each activity: "What I Was Good At" and "What I Struggled With." For each role, write down what activities or parts of your job you were especially good at, or not so good at:

- Did any particular projects stick out?
- Did you earn recognition for any accomplishments?
- Did you often receive praise for certain skills or qualities?

My Examples of What I Was Good At

Here is what I wrote down for the three jobs I mentioned before.

Grocery Bagger at Giant Eagle
(June 1999–August 1999)

What I Was Good At: I always arrived to work on time, I did what I was told to do (most of the time), and I got along with both customers and my co-workers.

What I Struggled With: I disliked doing the same task over and over again for four hours a day. Often, I would create games for myself to see how fast or efficiently I could pack the grocery bags. While this kept me entertained, it might not have been the most pleasant experience for the customer. I didn't enjoy standing on my feet for two to three hours at a time, and I did not like retrieving grocery carts in extremely hot weather.

Cashier at Shop 'n Save (March 2000–May 2000)

What I Was Good At: I always arrived on time. In addition, I provided customers with good service, even in the face of depressing working conditions.

What I Struggled With: I lost energy quickly because I disliked the work environment and did not engage with my colleagues.

Analyst at Wachovia (June 2005–May 2006)

What I Was Good At: I was able to create accurate, sophisticated models with Excel spreadsheets, and I developed clear stories around my analyses. I worked hard, demonstrated strong attention to detail, and studied on the weekends to expand my knowledge rapidly. I challenged the status quo and initiated new projects.

What I Struggled With: I grew up feeling like I always had to prove myself. In the workplace, that translated into being competitive with my fellow analysts, which did not create the best working dynamic. I also lacked confidence in my communication skills. As a result, I felt nervous about participating in meetings that involved senior executives.

After completing this exercise, review the activities and projects you noted under "What I Was Good At," and categorize them by type of interest or skill. Take note of any skills and interests that you discover before moving on. Here are some examples of categories to help you get started:

- **Communication Skills**: Write clear emails, communicate effectively internally and externally, develop engaging presentations, public speaking
- **Self-Management**: Hard-working, diligent, self-motivated, organized, proactive, efficient
- **Leadership**: Lead projects, speak up in meetings, suggest new projects or improvements to existing processes, help new or more junior co-workers
- **Interpersonal Skills**: Work well with internal and external stakeholders
- **Flexibility**: Ability to work under pressure, ability to adjust to changing priorities, able to work with little direction
- **Computer Skills**: Word processing, creating presentations, developing models, creating programs

Exercise 3: Your Outside Interests

(30–60 Minutes)

How do you spend your time outside of work? On your existing piece of paper or computer file, write down topics or subject areas you read about or listen to in your free time, whether via books, articles, blogs, podcasts, or videos. Do you see any common themes surrounding your interests?

For example, long before I became a financial planner, I would read about personal finance, real estate, and credit card hacking in my spare time. These topics interested me from both an intellectual and a practical perspective. As my knowledge level became more advanced, I began listening to personal finance podcasts on the subway. I'd regularly get into conversations about finance and real estate topics with anyone who was interested. Eventually, I began writing about personal finance topics on my blog. I even took vacation days to attend personal finance conferences (what a nerd!).

Exercise 4: Feedback from Others

(30 Minutes)

While reviewing your past experiences and current interests is a great start to figuring out what you like and what you're good at, sometimes talking to others can help you confirm what you already know or identify skills and interests you didn't even know you had. For this exercise, reach out to friends, co-workers (past and present), and family to help identify and confirm your skills and interests:

- Do people often reach out to you with particular questions?
- Do people frequently ask you for help on certain problems or projects?

I found this step to be especially helpful, and was able to identify several skills and interest areas that I had never thought of myself. For example, multiple friends told me I was really good at finding deals and optimizing my time – things I just assumed everyone was good at. A colleague said I had a talent for developing Excel models to help people make important life decisions – another skill that I had thought wasn't really unique to me. And my wife, Jennifer, specifically told me she thought I would be a great financial advisor.

It's easy now to look back and realize that becoming a financial planner was an obvious path. But in the moment, I thought that financial planning was a career for people who couldn't get into investment banking, and that the role just involved selling financial products. So my response to Jennifer in the moment was a firm no. Eight years later, here I am, writing to you as a proud financial planner.

Exercise 5: What Personality Tests Say

(30–60 Minutes)

Many work and personality tests are available to help you further uncover your interests and strengths, including the Myers-Briggs, StrengthsFinders, and DISC tests (all of which I have taken, and recommend). While these tests may not perfectly describe your personality or preferences, taken together with your past experiences and feedback from others, they can help confirm your interests and skills. Tests range in cost from $0 to $75, on average.

Part 2: Preferences and Priorities

With a better understanding of your interests and strengths, we next want to take a look at the type of job environment that may be a good fit based on your preferences and priorities.

Exercise 1: What You Want Life to Look Like

(30–60 Minutes)

One factor that I never took into account when considering my first job out of college was my desired lifestyle. That may have been because my classmates and I assumed college business majors had two career choices: investment banking or consulting. Since both routes required long work days and/or frequent travel, I thought having a stressful work experience was inevitable.

Seven years later, when I was contemplating leaving the investment banking industry for good, I was much more deliberate about ensuring that the next job I pursued met my lifestyle needs. By this point, I had a sense that many roles could align well with any particular set of skills and interests. I had also learned firsthand that regardless of how well you are doing professionally and financially, if your job prevents you from having the lifestyle you want, you likely aren't going to be happy. That's why this next exercise will focus on helping you determine what type of lifestyle is right for you.

Step 1: Envision Your Ideal Weekday and Weekend Day

It's time to forget about reality for a second and let yourself dream. Seriously, take a moment to think about what your ideal weekday and weekend day looks like from the moment you wake up to when you go to sleep. Don't think about how you would make your ideal days a reality – just think about what these ideal days would look like. On the sheet of paper or file you've been using, jot down as much detail as possible about how you would spend your days. While you don't have to name a specific job for weekdays (or weekend days), be sure to list skills you would like to be using or activities you would be doing (projects, meeting with clients, presentations, coding, design, etc.).

Consider answering the questions in Table 6.1 to help get you started (also available at www.workyourmoneybook.com).

Table 6.1   What Does Your Ideal Weekday and Weekend Day Look Like?

Question	Weekday	Weekend Day
1. What time would you wake up?		
2. What time would you go to sleep?		
3. How many hours of sleep would you get?		
4. How would your ideal morning start (having coffee in bed, working out, taking a yoga class)?		
5. What would you eat for breakfast, lunch, and dinner? Where would you be when you ate those meals? Would you cook them yourself, order in, or go to a restaurant?		
6. What activities would keep you engaged throughout the day?		
7. Who would you see during your ideal day? Would you talk with people on the phone, online, or via social media?		

Step 2: Consider Your Geographic Needs

Do you have a strong preference about where you want to live? If you can't think of a specific place, do you have a preference between living in a city, a suburb, or a small town, and on a broader scale, living in the US or in a different country? How important is it for you to live near friends or family? Take note of any location preferences you may have.

Step 3: Consider Your Financial Needs

Based on the work you did in Chapters 4 and 5, how much money do you need to make to support your current or desired lifestyle? Think about what your initial salary requirement may be, the salary you want to make in the long term, your preference for the type of compensation received (e.g., salary, bonus, stock), and any required benefits needed (e.g., 401(k) matching, health plan). Write these notes on your existing sheet or file.

Exercise 2: What Trade-Offs You're Willing to Make

(20–30 Minutes)

There are always consequences and trade-offs when you make decisions about how to allocate time between your personal and professional lives. The following questions focus on what work-life trade-offs you may be willing to make. Take your time formulating your responses; they may require quite a bit of thought:

- How flexible are you on a specific city or location? If you could make more money in a location other than your ideal location, would you make that trade-off? If so, how much more money would you have to earn?
- Are you willing to work in a high-pressure job that requires you to work evenings, and sometimes weekends? Would you be

willing to be on call or available to your team 24/7? How much of a salary increase would you need to make this trade-off?

- How often are you willing to travel in a job? Are you willing to travel most weekdays, like a typical consultant, or do you prefer not to travel at all? Would money play a role in the amount of time you were willing to travel?
- Is it important to you to eat dinner at home every night, whether alone or with your family (pets included!)?

Piecing Together Your Ideal Job

When you've finished all of the exercises in this chapter, review your answers to see if you can identify key themes from your responses. Use Table 6.2 and the questions below to help you organize and hone your thoughts (the table is also available at www.workyourmoneybook .com).

Once you've done so, another helpful tactic, according to Blair Decembrele, Director of Global Marketing Communications and Career Expert at LinkedIn, could be to use that information to write your ideal job description. "It's a practice that some companies are starting to enlist to attract top talent. This exercise could help you further uncover whether your current job is fulfilling your needs, or if it's time to renegotiate your position or look for a new opportunity elsewhere, maybe even in an entirely new industry."

Questions to Consider

- Can you confirm or eliminate certain industries or positions from your list (maybe even your current role or industry), based on one or more of the following factors?
  - **Quality of Life**: If you value having a significant amount of personal time, you may be able to eliminate certain jobs right off the bat – like investment banking or law. Similarly, if you don't want to travel, then an on-the-road career like management consulting is probably not the right fit for you.

- **Location**: If proximity to your family is important to you, you might choose to target jobs in a particular city or region. On the other hand, if you're open to moving, you may be able to expand the types of work you're considering.
- **Compensation**: Based on your compensation requirements, you may be able to eliminate certain industries or roles.
- **Content**: Consider whether any roles or industries you've identified may be a good fit, based on the strengths and interests you've noted. If you're outgoing and appreciate the art of the deal, for instance, then maybe a sales role is right down your alley.

Table 6.2 Summary of Desired Job Preferences.

Type of Role	
Functional Area (sales, operations, product management, engineering, trading, etc.)	
Internally or Externally Facing	
Individual Contributor or Manager	
Proactive or Reactive Work	
Lifestyle	
Target Location(s)	
Work Hours	
Stress Level	
Compensation & Benefits	
Target All-In Salary	
Required Employee Benefits (401(k) matching, health benefits, etc.)	

Table 6.2   (*continued*)

Job Functions	
To Consider	To Eliminate
Industries	
To Consider	To Eliminate

Chapter 7
How to Tweak Your Job

Have you ever felt so stressed or unhappy at work that you thought you needed to do something extreme to fix the situation, like quit your job, travel the world, pursue very early retirement, or all of the above? Been there, done that. Whenever I used to have a bad week at work, I'd be quick to think about making a major change. Drastic times call for drastic measures, right?

Over the years, what I've come to realize is that the solution to remedy non-ideal work situations doesn't have to be severe at all. Many times, small changes in your role can significantly improve how you feel about your job and your overall quality of life.

Tweaking your current job may be easier than you think and generally involves less risk, less time, and a lower upfront monetary investment than other strategies, which is why I recommend using this strategy as a first step. Cara Brennan Allamano, Senior Vice President of Human Resources at Udemy, says, "No matter what role you're in, own your performance and how you can impact the business."

What Do You Mean By "Tweak"?

When you began your current job, you probably inherited a job description that included an outline of your responsibilities. These tasks were likely assigned based on what a prior employee did in your role. While your initial job description is a fine place to start – especially while you're still getting up to speed in a new role and company – it can and should change over the duration of your employment. New skill sets are often needed as businesses and industries evolve and innovate. Your role should also reflect your strengths and interests, which may differ from those of your predecessor.

That's where job tweaking comes in. Think of this process as less about trying to shirk or avoid certain tasks, and more about better matching your job responsibilities with your strengths. Job tweaking could include transitioning some tasks to others, taking on new responsibilities, or changing the timing of certain day-to-day work.

Dr. Amy Wrzesniewski of Yale University, Dr. Jane Dutton of the University of Michigan, and Dr. Justin Berg of Stanford University have conducted numerous studies on tweaking your job, or what they call "job crafting."[1] Their research subjects have included employees of varying occupations, at different levels, and in organizations ranging from Fortune 500 companies to small nonprofits. What they found is that employees who try tweaking their jobs "often end up more engaged and satisfied with their work lives, achieving higher levels of performance in their organizations, and report greater personal resilience."

Table 7.1 provides a number of common situations where job tweaking may be beneficial.

Getting Started

While the prospect of tweaking your job or asking your manager if you can adjust your role may sound scary, it doesn't have to be. Brennan Allamano notes, "Jobs are being tweaked constantly, whether or not managers or companies are endorsing or directing

Table 7.1   Situations Where a Job Tweak Could Help.

Situation	Potential Tweaks
Your responsibilities don't align with your skills and interests.	• Could you take on other responsibilities or projects on your current team (either now or gradually) that better align with your skills and interests?
You feel like you are micromanaged, lack much decision-making power, and are just completing someone else's to-do list.	• Could you bring up to your manager your preferred working style and suggest a test period for receiving more autonomy?
You lack direction about how you can be effective in your role.	• Could you meet with your manager to clarify your responsibilities and their expectations of you? • Could you arrange periodic meetings throughout the year to check in on your progress and performance?
You aren't gaining the exposure or new skills you need that could help you eventually transition to other internal or external roles.	• Could you take on additional projects (either on or outside of your current team) that would expose you to other people in your organization and help you build skills that will increase your competitiveness in the job market?
You feel burned out and/or guilty about taking time off.	• Could you take actions to help create boundaries between your work and personal time (e.g., better manage expectations with stakeholders, give yourself longer deadlines to complete projects, and/or avoid taking on work outside of your areas of responsibility or expertise?) • Could you set up time with co-workers to discuss their strategies for balancing their schedules?
You receive a lot of reactive and last-minute requests, even on nights and weekends.	• Do the reactive and last-minute requests often come from the same person? If so, have you tried managing expectations with this person by letting them know that you typically need a certain amount of lead time to be able to do a good job?
You believe you are being underpaid and/or are being promoted slower than others with similar experience and a similar performance history.	• Could you speak to your manager about your accomplishments and the reasons you believe you deserve a raise or promotion? • If your company runs a more rigid process for salary increases or promotions, do you also feel comfortable talking to your manager about what you both need to do to make it happen?

that process." That being said, it probably doesn't make sense to start tweaking your role from day one in your job. Your attempt to tweak your job is much more likely to succeed if you've been in your role for some time and have clearly demonstrated value to your team and company.

So how do you get started? Here is a recommended roadmap, based on my personal experiences and those of others.

Step 1: Think of Solutions, Not Just Problems

Your manager probably has a lot on their plate already. They'll likely be less receptive to your request if you come to them complaining about your current responsibilities, because they may feel like you are simply creating more work for them. On the other hand, if you identify concrete changes that could improve your situation or better yet, additional ways you can add value, your manager may feel less overwhelmed by the need to come up with a solution – which will likely make them more amenable to helping you achieve your goals.

Fran Hauser, former President of Digital at Time, Inc. and author of *The Myth of the Nice Girl*, suggests identifying organizational gaps and ways you can make your boss's life easier to come up with possible solutions. This approach helped Hauser gain responsibility quickly and accelerate her career trajectory. And as a boss, she appreciated it when her reports came to her to volunteer for a specific task.

"I was always so grateful anytime one of my team members proactively offered to take a first stab at a report or presentation I had to do," she says. "Often times, it led to them being included in the meeting where the report was being presented, and in the process, gaining valuable exposure and knowledge."

Step 2: Think Win-Win

As you craft solutions for tweaking your current role, think about how you can make any change a win-win solution for both you and the organization.

"Determine what you want and why, come up with a game plan with how you're going to get it that relates to the business goals, and then work backwards from there. If you have a well thought out strategy that shows what's good for the business and you, that makes it hard for your manager to say no," says Lauren McGoodwin, founder of Career Contessa.

Step 3: Present Your Case to Your Manager

Once you've come up with concrete proposals that will be a win-win for everyone in the organization, set up a meeting with your manager to discuss your ideas. The discussion doesn't need to be anything formal, but do keep in mind your manager's preferences and communication style. Blair Decembrele, Director of Global Marketing Communications and Career Expert at LinkedIn, says, "Consider how your manager best processes information, and how they measure success. If they're data-driven, consider including some research and performance metrics with your case. If your manager is more subjective, you may want to paint the picture by sharing your contributions and workplace performance."

Never threaten to leave your job if your request can't be met (even if that might be your intention). Instead, keep the tone positive and goal-oriented.

How Others Made It Happen

Megan's Story

Megan joined a top technology company as a sales analyst a year ago, and finally feels like she has a decent understanding of her role, and does it well.

However, there are some blurry areas that have become a pain point for her. In particular, Megan frequently receives requests from other teams that may not be her responsibility. Because she is still relatively new, Megan has been taking on these requests in an effort to build a strong reputation. However, the additional work is preventing Megan from being able to focus on her main projects, causing her to finish her own work at night and on weekends. Megan is stressed about how to manage everything and keep it together.

At the encouragement of her friends, Megan decides to bring up the situation with her manager. Megan asks her manager whether they can work with other teams to develop clearer swim lanes. Megan's manager thinks that is a great idea, and arranges a meeting with other managers to clarify everyone's responsibilities. Megan is invited to attend the meeting, and shares several suggestions for how to manage and reroute requests across teams.

As a result of the meeting, Megan feels empowered to assign misdirected ad hoc requests she receives to the proper team, allowing her to focus on her core responsibilities. She no longer has to work on nights and weekends, and feels much less stressed. Because of her role in the managers' meeting, Megan has expanded her network among senior-level colleagues.

Takeaways

- If you have a question about your role or responsibilities, speak up. Chances are, the issue has not been considered and it might even affect others in the organization as well.
- Helping to identify and solve problems can lead to opportunities for you.

Rick's Story

Rick has worked at a leading social media platform for five years as an advertising salesperson. His main role is to work with advertisers to secure advertising space on his employer's website. A natural people person, Rick is often wining and dining clients when not wowing them with beautiful presentations.

While Rick really enjoys his job and his company, he's ready to shift to more strategic work. The problem is, most of the internal job board listings require Excel and project management skills that he lacks.

After doing some research online, Rick finds a weeklong Excel bootcamp he can participate in. Although the program typically targets investment bankers, he decides to enroll anyhow. The course helps reinforce Rick's desire to change roles. While he's still in the process of landing a new role, he feels much more qualified to be able to apply for internal strategy positions now that he's taken the Excel course.

Takeaways

- There are so many ways to gain new skills these days. With a little bit of research and a can-do attitude, it can be relatively easy to fill in the skills gap on your resume.

Jen's Story

Jen has worked at a Fortune 500 company for four years as a financial analyst. She thinks her job is interesting and really likes her colleagues, but she often feels overwhelmed and anxious. Jen finds herself working on most nights and weekends, unlike most of her co-workers.

After meeting with a career coach and separately with a therapist, Jen realizes her demanding schedule may be self-inflicted. She feels that she has to constantly prove herself or else she may not be valuable to the company.

Upon coming to this realization, Jen starts to institute new habits to promote mindfulness and well-being, including 1) not checking her work email after 8 p.m. on weekdays and throughout the weekend, 2) not working on weeknights or weekends unless it's absolutely necessary, 3) beginning to meditate, 4) eating healthier, and 5) checking her email less throughout the workday. While she's only been doing this for two months, she can already feel a weight lifted off her shoulders.

Takeaways

- It's important to identify when stressful work schedules are externally driven versus self-inflicted, to know how to remedy the situation. Internally driven stress will not decrease by changing external circumstances, such as your actual job or company.
- It can be valuable to seek out unbiased service providers to help see the forest from the trees. In this case, career coaches, life coaches, or therapists may help give you perspective.

Jamie's Story

Jamie, a marketing specialist at a leading credit card company, has consistently received excellent reviews and ratings for the past four years without being promoted. She feels demoralized and confused about what else she can do to advance, especially because other colleagues in her role who joined the company at the same time as her have received promotions.

At the advice of a career mentor, Jamie decides to meet with her manager to discuss the promotion process. She explains that being promoted is an important growth milestone for her, and asks what else she needs to do to advance to the next level. Her boss, who is still a relatively new manager, tells Jamie she'll schedule a follow-up meeting to discuss next steps after speaking with senior management.

In the follow-up meeting, Jamie's manager tells her that senior management feels she needs to show more leadership qualities to get promoted. As a result, Jamie and her manager develop a plan for how she can develop her leadership skills by initiating and overseeing new projects that will expose her to senior leaders. They also set up a recurring monthly meeting to discuss and track Jamie's progress.

As a result of this action plan, Jamie receives a promotion at the end of the year. She feels much more valued, and is now consistently assigned to the most high-profile projects.

Takeaways

- You have to take an active role in career management and development.
- Promotion processes can vary greatly from company to company, and across industries. Speak to your manager to get clarity on the process and expectations, so you know exactly what it takes to proceed to the next level.

Your Turn

Refer back to the job analysis table you completed in Chapter 3 and pay close attention to the obstacles you identified. What actions could you take to "tweak" your role and gradually eliminate them? You can use Table 7.2 to gather your thoughts (the table is also available as a template at www.workyourmoneybook.com).

When Is a Job Tweak Not Enough?

This chapter focused on strategies that can help you identify ways to tweak your role, so that you can gain increased job satisfaction based on the preferences you identified. But sometimes, a job tweak simply doesn't cut it.

For example, if you feel generally satisfied with your job, but are less excited about your industry and day-to-day responsibilities, you may choose not only to tweak your current job but also to add another role. Or if your job has more fundamental issues, you may want to change it up entirely.

Table 7.2 Brainstorming Ways to Tweak Your Job.

Work Factor	Translation	Obstacles	Potential Ways to Eliminate Obstacles
1. Are You Getting Value?	Do you like what you do on a day-to-day basis?		
2. Are You Adding Value?	Do you feel you're able to make an impact in your job?		
3. Are You Increasing Your Value in the Market?	Does your current role expand or decrease your future job options?		
4. Does Your Role Align with Your Values?	Do your office environment, work schedule flexibility, and employee benefits improve your overall quality of life?		
5. Do You Feel Valued?	Do you feel like you are being fairly rewarded through pay, promotions, and work responsibilities?		

In the next chapter, we'll dive into how to supplement your current role with another job to help fulfill unmet job needs, explore potential career paths, or both.

Chapter 8

Supplement Your Job to Explore New Opportunities

Slash careers. Side hustles. 20% projects. Whatever you choose to call them, more people than ever are supplementing their primary jobs with a second gig. In fact, according to a 2018 Bankrate.com report, nearly 4 in 10 Americans work more than one job.[1]

Extra cash isn't the only reason why people are increasingly pursuing side hustles. Many side hustlers use additional projects to fulfill their creative needs. For example, I've met people who have started photography, writing, and Etsy businesses on the side to develop artistic talents that they don't use in their regular day jobs. Other side hustles serve as testing grounds for potential full-time gigs. In his book *The 10% Entrepreneur*, author Patrick McGinnis highlights many successful business leaders whose ventures began as side projects, including Luke Holden, founder of the popular seafood chain Luke's Lobster.[2] Holden initially launched the business while working as a Wall Street analyst. What began as a

200-square-foot hole-in-the-wall lobster shack has since grown into a global enterprise that generates tens of millions in annual sales.

The Perks

Side hustles might be an attractive and highly effective strategy if you are looking to gain more satisfaction in your professional life. Among the many benefits, supplementing your current job can allow you to:

- **Safely Test Drive New Areas**: Quitting your job to explore new areas may be extremely stressful and financially infeasible. But by pursuing a side hustle, you can try out new career paths or passions with the safety and security of your existing job. This way, you don't have to worry about making money immediately and can simply focus on whether you enjoy other key elements of the work.
- **Explore Entrepreneurship**: Starting a side hustle can provide you an opportunity to explore whether you would like entrepreneurship and being your own boss. We all hear about the potential upsides of owning a business, but starting a side hustle allows you to see for yourself, in a relatively risk-free environment, whether you would enjoy the ups and downs of overseeing all aspects of a business.
- **Gain New Skills**: Taking on a side hustle may allow you to gain new skills that you are unable to build or hone in your day job.
- **Satisfy Unmet Job Needs**: In Chapter 3, you analyzed the key job areas for your existing role. A side hustle may allow you to address those areas that were less positive – some of which may be impossible to improve otherwise, based on the realities of your role, organization, or industry. For example, if you dislike the basic content of your job but enjoy other aspects, you may be able to find a more engaging subject matter through a side hustle.

- **Earn Extra Money**: In the long term, taking on a side hustle allows you to explore new areas and gain real-world insights into which paths may be most viable. But in the meantime, your side hustle may also allow you to supplement your income so that you can improve your quality of life or help achieve your personal financial goals.
- **Meet New People**: A side hustle can also allow you to expand your network. In particular, you'll likely develop new connections both online and in person through the process of researching, building, and marketing your side hustle. These new contacts could become mentors, partners, allies, or even friends.
- **Diversify Your Life**: Adding a side hustle allows you to diversify your life, which may help you reduce your exposure to just one employer. That's important because putting all of your eggs in one basket can be risky from both a financial and an emotional perspective. For example, if you are receiving negative energy or feedback in your day job on a particular day, other activities may help you feel more balanced and even-keeled, decreasing the likelihood of experiencing severe lows.

My Experience Diversifying My Life

In my finance days, I did the exact opposite of diversification. Instead, most of my life revolved around my job – in terms of time and energy.

Having my life concentrate so much on work meant that how well I did in my job on a particular day dictated my mood. If I received positive feedback on my contributions to a project, I would feel euphoric. On the other hand, if I was criticized for any reason, big or small, I would often become despondent.

(continued)

(*continued*)

Unfortunately, I was overexposed to the whims of my job with nothing else to balance out my life. Based on that experience, I've since become a huge proponent of diversifying your life. That's one of the reasons why I choose to work at Google, run a financial planning firm, and participate in a range of activities that keep me busy, entertained, and engaged. If one area of my life isn't going well, I can usually derive satisfaction from another area to help balance out my emotional state. As a result, I rarely feel extreme lows on a particular day. And that's the way I like it.

Now, Some Practical Points

While there are many benefits to starting a side hustle, you should consider certain practical points before hanging up your shingle. In particular, keep in mind that in a side hustle:

- **You Need Time**: Blogs and articles often make having a side hustle sound so easy. But the truth is, researching, building, and marketing a new venture takes time. Extra time is something most of us don't have, so you'll need to create a schedule of your typical week and then ask yourself:
  - Which of the activities that currently take up my time are required (such as working my day job or spending time with my family), and which ones are voluntary (for example, binge-watching Netflix shows or playing fantasy football)?
  - Which voluntary activities would I be willing to forgo in order to pursue a side hustle?

- Am I efficiently using my time right now? Are there ways I can fit in a side hustle without devoting less time to my current personal and professional activities? (For more tips on this topic, refer to Chapter 15.)
- **You Won't See Immediate Results**: While you'll need to commit a certain number of hours each week to your side hustle, you won't see immediate results or receive positive reinforcement right away, which can be frustrating. Some of the most successful bloggers often talk about how when they originally launched their sites, they had maybe 10 visitors to their sites a day, which consisted of their own visits and some family.
- **You May Need Extra Money**: Starting a side hustle often involves a number of steps. For example, you may need additional training before you can begin actually side hustling in your target area. Even when you attain the necessary qualifications to begin a venture, you may need to cover certain administrative costs, such as buying a website domain name and hosting services for your website, printing business cards, investing in advertising, and registering your business, among other costs.
- **A Side Hustle Shouldn't Threaten Your Current Job Prospects**: One of the benefits of the side hustle route is that it provides you the opportunity to experiment professionally while still enjoying the stability of a regular paycheck. A key to making this strategy work is to avoid activities or commitments that would jeopardize the security of your day job. That means:
  - Prioritize your day job first. Make sure you're still completing your tasks well and on time.
  - Don't use your company's resources to benefit your side hustle. For example, refrain from working on your side hustle while at the office, using your work computer for your side hustle, or advertising your side hustle to work clients.

- Check your company's code of conduct, conflict of interest, communications, and moonlighting policies, to make sure you understand the in-bounds and out-of-bounds activities for your potential side hustle.

Getting Started: Figure Out What to Pursue and Make It a Reality

Launching a side hustle begins with quite a bit of research, reflection, and planning. Although this stage can feel tedious, it is arguably the most important part of the process. By carefully considering the many factors that will impact your side hustle, you will be able to identify foreseeable deal breakers and obstacles before getting too far along. The prelaunch phase includes the following steps.

Determine Your "Why"

Define what you want from a side hustle by thinking about the following:

- **Purpose of Side Hustle**: Is the purpose of launching a side hustle to 1) fulfill unmet job needs, 2) explore a new professional area, 3) earn extra cash, 4) a combination of the above, or 5) something else?
- **Type of Side Hustle**: Do you hope to make enough money from your side hustle to cover your operational costs plus perhaps a little extra (i.e., a hobby), or do you aspire to eventually replace your day job income with your side hustle earnings?

Explore Areas to Pursue

With your "why" in mind, you can start exploring the many possible paths for you to pursue. Some people may already have a side hustle they've been thinking about for a long time, and know they'd like to pursue that area. For everyone else, the following factors can help you focus on a few areas:

- **Reflect on Your Past Work**: You may be able to leverage a lot of the work you've already done in Chapters 3 and 6, where you identified missing elements of your current role, as well as the elements of your ideal role. Refer back to your work so you can refresh your memory on the interests and skills you pinpointed that are important to you, as well as topics or subject areas in which people often come to you for answers. Review what books, articles, or blogs you read in your spare time. All of this past work can give you hints about potential focus areas for your side hustle.
- **Find Existing Case Studies**: Next, you can perform online research to learn about types of side hustles from relevant industries that have proved successful. This approach may be especially important if you are embarking on a side hustle with the hope of creating a long-term business that eventually becomes your full-time job. Remember that a side hustle could either be broad in nature or highly specialized. Some examples of broad-based side hustles include blogging, freelance writing, consulting, teaching, tutoring, and advising – all of which you could customize for one or more areas of interest. Other side hustles focus on a single subject area or vertical, such as rental real estate management or fashion design.
- **Explore Business Models**: As you consider what area to pursue in your side hustle, you'll also want to figure out how you'll make money. Generally, you can generate revenue by: 1) selling your products, 2) selling your services, or 3) selling other people's/companies' products or services. Refer to Table 8.1 for some examples of these business models.

Consider Your Funding Strategy

Nearly all side hustles require at least some upfront financial investment. Once you've determined the area(s) you'd like to pursue, you will need to estimate how much your side hustle will

Table 8.1   Potential Business Models for Side Hustles.

Business Model	Examples
1. Sell your products.	• Handcrafts in an Etsy store • eBook
2. Sell your services.	• Web design services • Career coaching services • Financial planning services
3. Sell other people's products or services.	• Display advertising • Sponsored content • Affiliate advertising

cost on an upfront and ongoing basis. You can do this in several ways, including:

- **Search the Internet**: I've found that running a couple of targeted online searches is typically a good starting point for estimating your costs. Often you'll find several articles outlining startup costs for various types of side hustles, based on other people's firsthand experience.
- **Reach out to Industry Experts:** After completing some preliminary research, you may wish to contact other people who have successfully launched the types of businesses you're considering. Reaching out to industry experts can help you verify your online research, improve your understanding of the likely costs, and even provide you tricks or tools for funding your business. I took this very approach when I was considering whether to launch my financial planning firm. After conducting a lot of online research, I contacted several financial planners in New York City to learn about the process they went through to fund and develop their business, the amount of time it took, the service providers they used, and any other helpful tips they would be willing to share.
- **Enlist a Business Coach**: When starting a new venture, a business coach could help you decrease the amount of online

research you need to do to get started. In addition, coaches can brainstorm your potential venture with you, and for ongoing relationships, hold you accountable. Once your business is started, a coach may be able to give you suggestions on how to streamline your operations, and help you think about how to expand to new markets or clients.

Take Action

While you may have researched multiple side hustles, you should be ready to choose the initiative that most excites you now and is also viable. Since you'll already be taking away time from other personal activities, it's best to start with one side hustle and see how it works within your life rather than attempt multiple ventures. Evaluating your interest in a particular side hustle is much more difficult if you're stressed, overextended, and burned out.

Once you've selected a side hustle, develop a six-month to one-year plan that outlines what a "good" outcome looks like for you at the end of your initial testing period. A "good" outcome could include a concrete or quantifiable goal you would like to achieve, such as a revenue target, client goal, or education and skills milestone. Make sure to translate your large goal into bite-sized actions that you can complete on a weekly or monthly basis.

You'll also need to find the time to work on your new project. At a minimum, you should aim to work on your side hustle several hours a week. For me, on the weekdays, early mornings between 7 and 9 a.m., and after work between 6 and 8 p.m., are when I've mentally made time for my various side hustles. I prefer working on my side hustles in the early morning because I typically am relatively refreshed from the night before and reactive requests or fire drills have not come in yet from my day job. On the weekends, I typically spend a couple of hours in the morning at a coffee shop working on my side hustle. This small amount of time has allowed me to try out real estate, freelance writing, financial planning, and now, writing a book!

Use Table 8.2 as a guide to get you started on mapping out your side hustle (also available at www.workyourmoneybook.com).

Table 8.2   Sample Side Hustle Six-Month Plan for Real Estate Agent.

Six-Month Goal	• Become a licensed real estate agent. • Secure one buyer client.
Monthly Actions/Goals	
Month 1	• Research requirements to become a real estate agent. • Reach out to other part-time real estate agents to understand how they were able to start and grow their business. • Enroll in online real estate licensing course.
Month 2	• Complete online real estate licensing course. • Study and pass state licensing exam.
Month 3	• Research and decide on real estate brokerage. • Create marketing materials, including business cards, LinkedIn announcement, and email announcement to network. • Write and pitch real estate blog post/article to bloggers and notable websites.
Month 4	• Lead one speaking engagement on how to buy an apartment in New York City to try to secure new clients. • Network with at least one established real estate agent to try to secure referral clients for prospects that may not be a fit for their business.
Month 5	• Lead one speaking engagement on how to buy an apartment in New York City to try to secure new clients. • Network with at least one established real estate agent to try to secure referral clients for prospects that may not be a fit for their business.
Month 6	• Lead one speaking engagement on how to buy an apartment in New York City to try to secure new clients. • Network with at least one established real estate agent to try to secure referral clients for prospects that may not be a fit for their business.

Table 8.2   (*continued*)

Side Hustle Working Time		
Weekdays	• **Monday:**	7:00 a.m. to 8:30 a.m.
	• **Tuesday:**	7:00 a.m. to 8:30 a.m.
	• **Wednesday:**	7:00 a.m. to 8:30 a.m.
	• **Thursday:**	7:00 a.m. to 8:30 a.m.
	• **Friday:**	7:00 a.m. to 8:30 a.m.
Weekends	• **Saturday:**	10:00 a.m. to 12:00 p.m.
	• **Sunday:**	10:00 a.m. to 12:00 p.m.
Where Will Time Come From?	• Move workouts from 7:00 a.m. on weekdays to 6:00 p.m. • Decrease amount of time watching television, Netflix, and live sports.	
How Will You Make Sure You Stick to Your Plan?	• Put allotted side hustle time into my calendar. • Let my wife know of my plan and make sure she is on board.	

Evaluate and Make Adjustments

You're not going to like every activity you participate in, which is totally natural. The great thing about side hustles is that they allow you to dip your toe in the water of potential interest areas and gain a better sense of the day-to-day skills required to be successful, without needing to take the risks that a job change typically requires.

In order to maximize the benefits of a side hustle, you should reflect on your feelings periodically and make adjustments as necessary. That might mean deciding that a side hustle that you originally thought could someday be your full-time job would be better as a hobby. Or you might choose to ditch the side hustle entirely because you've realized you don't enjoy it after all.

Brock McGoff – founder of the Modest Man, a website dedicated to helping shorter men dress better – tried a side hustle in music production and developed a number of websites, before pushing forward with the Modest Man concept. He says, "Building niche websites was a great way to learn about content development, but I wasn't passionate about any of them. I was just working on those particular sites for the money, which I realized wouldn't be sustainable or fulfilling in the long term. As I started to get more into menswear and dressing better, I decided to create a website with content around what I would have wanted to read about men's style." After working on the site for three years as a side hustle, McGoff made the leap and turned the Modest Man into his main gig – and he hasn't looked back since.

Alternatively, you could start off by pursuing a side hustle as a hobby, discover unexpected success, and eventually consider whether to make it your full-time job. That's exactly what happened to Jim Wang, who created a personal finance website called Bargaineering in 2005 while working as a software engineer. "I always had an interest in personal finance and how it worked, so I started the blog to help me understand it. I never thought it'd become something that other people would want to read." But within just a couple years, Wang saw his Bargaineering earnings climb to $30,000. The website's rapid growth prompted Wang to rethink whether he should pursue Bargaineering as "just a hobby." By 2008, with the site generating six-figure earnings, Wang decided to make Bargaineering his full-time gig. "When I was thinking about whether to go all-in, one concern was how long blogging as a business could last," Wang explains. "But I decided that regardless of the staying power, I would look back with regret if I didn't devote all of my energy to growing the site." Five years after launching Bargaineering, Wang sold the site for a multimillion-dollar payout. He is now developing another personal finance-focused website called Wallet Hacks.

Neil Pasricha, bestselling author of *The Book of Awesome* and *The Happiness Equation*, and Director of the Institute of Global Happiness, also saw his side hustle evolve over time in unexpected ways. He began writing and speaking while serving as Director of Leadership Development at Walmart. Initially, Pasricha had no plans to transition either side hustle into a full-time gig. He explains, "Writers write something like 1.1 books on average, so after I finished my first book, I thought that would be my 15 minutes of fame – end of story. When it came to speaking, I had heard that the average speaking career lasts about six years, which sounded way too short to quit a steady day job. I also appreciated the benefits that my day job provided me, including a sense of structure and a place to socialize with others."

But Pasricha's feelings changed after six years of writing and speaking on the side. He reevaluated his situation and ultimately decided to leave his job at Walmart in order to give his side gigs his full attention. Pasricha says, "Part of my decision was personal – having kids took time away from nights and weekends when I would typically work on my writing and speaking. And part of my decision was seeing the viability of both – after writing five books and participating in 150 speaking engagements, I thought I could actually do these activities for a living."

Deciding Whether to Go All-In

While many of the stories highlighted involve people who eventually turned their side hustles into their full-time jobs, the decision to make that leap should not be taken lightly. Many did so only after balancing their day jobs and side hustles for several years, and Pasricha believes there are many benefits to doing this balancing act as long as possible. "I believe having multiple things going on somewhat counterintuitively enables you to take more risk in each! For example, if you have a weekend wedding DJ business that you could see yourself leaning into, you might feel more empowered to speak up at your day job, which, of course, helps you get noticed and promoted more. And if you have a day job, then you may feel free to take more risks in your art."

Financially, you'll also want to run the numbers to evaluate whether turning your side hustle into your main gig is feasible. Ask yourself the following questions:

- Do the net revenues from your side hustle cover your living expenses, which you outlined in Chapters 4 and 5? Make sure to adjust your living expenses upward for any expenses that may be artificially lower because of your employee benefits, such as health care costs.

- In a base case scenario, staying on your current trajectory, where would you shake out with net revenues in one year? What would net revenues look like in the best-case scenario? What about in a worst-case scenario?
- What if you quit your job, make your side hustle your full-time job and the worst-case scenario happens – what would you do? Can you stomach that worst-case scenario?

Chapter 9
Prepare to Change Your Job

In Chapters 7 and 8, we explored how to tweak or supplement a job, both of which can be effective, low-risk strategies for attaining more career or life satisfaction. But sometimes, those two options simply don't cut it. In fact, I've worked with several people who literally thought their job was making them ill. Even in less extreme cases, it may make sense to switch jobs entirely rather than hoping a small change in your current work situation will do the trick. In this chapter, we'll discuss whether a complete job change might be your best choice, and if so, how you can go about landing your next role.

Should You Stay, or Should You Go?

A job change could make sense if work factors you value are missing in your current role, if there is a big gap between your current job and the ideal job you identified in Chapter 6, or if you've identified another position that may be a better fit through a job tweak or side hustle.

Think back to the exercises you did in Chapter 3 to evaluate your current job. If the work factors you prioritized as most important aren't being adequately satisfied and you've been unsuccessful in trying to tweak those aspects of your job, that may be a sign that it's time to look for a new role. If you don't like your current industry or your day-to-day work, and lack the time or mental energy to add more responsibilities through a side hustle, then finding another role may be the way to go. And certainly, if your job makes you feel less than stellar physically and/or mentally, that could be another important signal that you should seek a new position.

Your financial resources and how much money you're willing to commit to a job search are another factor to consider. You may need to draw on your savings to fund networking activities, enlist a career coach, or enroll in classes to build new skills.

Focus Your Search

While a complete job change may be appropriate for your situation, focusing your search can help you greatly improve the chances of landing the role you want. Initially, it may give you a sense of accomplishment to use a "spray and pray" approach and cast your net widely – that is, apply for as many different types of jobs as you can. However, the opposite is actually true. Indeed, a search engine for job listings, found that people who submitted the most job applications were much less likely to receive a positive response from employers – 39% less likely.[1] Undertaking an overly broad job search not only hurts your chances of getting a response from employers, but it also decreases the likelihood of landing a role that *actually* aligns with what you want to do.

Using a more targeted approach allows you to show employers that you've invested time and thought into your search, makes it easier for you to market yourself to employers, and helps you align your efforts with roles that fit your interests, skills, and desired lifestyle. That's why by the end of this chapter, you will have narrowed down your possible roles to pursue to one or two.

Step 1: Explore Through Online Research

The first step to closing in on a target role is mapping out all of the possibilities, which means creating a list of potential industries, companies, and job functions. There are a number of strategies you could use to start your exploration. If you've already identified the particular job function you'd like to pursue, then your research may revolve around figuring out which industries and companies have a need for those roles. On the other hand, if you aren't tied to a specific job function, you may start by researching industries and companies that seem interesting to you, and then identify specific roles and job functions where your skills may be in demand. This approach may work for those still in college or professionals who have skills that could be applied across a number of different roles.

Lauren McGoodwin, founder of Career Contessa, encourages job seekers to focus on finding the right company rather than overemphasizing the specific role. "Know that you are smart and that you can do a lot of different things in your career. You're going to be switching jobs a lot – all the statistics say so. If you focus on working for a company that aligns with your values and that offers the benefits that are important to you, you can be the person that changes jobs a lot within that company, which is much easier than changing companies completely. That may serve you better in the long term."

To start exploring, use any or all of the following strategies, together with leveraging the summary of your job preferences, which you completed at the end of Chapter 6.

Research Possible Roles

When exploring roles, ask yourself, "Which roles may align with my skills and interests?"

- **LinkedIn Profiles**: Perform an advanced search on LinkedIn for people who had a similar role at your company or at competitors, to see the roles they've been able to transition to. This could help you understand the types of job functions that may value your skills and experience.

- **Job Descriptions**: Review job descriptions for different roles to see the type of jobs where you meet all of the *must-have* education, experience, and skill requirements. "Job descriptions often contain a laundry list of nice-to-have items that the hiring manager wishes the ideal candidate would possess, but they rarely expect a candidate to actually have *all* of those. Your job is to try to identify the core requirements for each role you review," says Amanda Augustine, career expert at TopResume, a resume-writing service. Depending on the amount of financial runway you have or are willing to build up, as well as the amount of time you're willing to devote to a transition, you may also want to review and consider roles where you only meet some of the must-have requirements.
- **Online Searches**: Do online searches to find lists, articles, or job listings that would value your core skill set. For example, someone who has strong analytical skills may search for "jobs that require analytical skills." This research could give you more ideas on the types of roles that could match your skills.

Explore Possible Companies

When researching companies, ask yourself, "Which companies may align with my career objectives, values, and desired lifestyle?"

- **Company Career Sections**: Review the employment section of company websites to understand company size, organizational structure, available positions, profiles of current employees, and hiring practices.
- **Recent News Articles**: Do a search for news articles about target companies to get a better understanding of recent company developments and the financial health of the company. This will help you grasp whether the company is involved in initiatives that interest you, as well as if the company is on an upward, downward, or flat trajectory.
- **Job-Specific Sites and Forums**: Look at job-specific sites, like `glassdoor.com` or `vault.com`, or even forums such as `reddit.com`, to get the scoop on how employees feel about their

companies. Be careful not to jump to conclusions based on one or two reviews. As with other review sites, if there are very few reviews for a company, chances are you'll get a skewed point of view from someone who has either a very positive or negative view of the company.

My Experience Exploring Potential Careers

When I was looking to transition from investment banking, I started my exploration by mapping out possible roles into two lists – one for financial services roles, and another for nonfinancial services roles. My goal was to lay out all of my options, including those roles that were closely related to my recent experience and those completely unrelated to what I had been doing.

My list for financial roles included the job functions I was interested in, such as investment banking, investment management, private equity, and venture capital. I used a different segmentation method for the nonfinancial roles list because, based on my research, I got the sense that company size (e.g., small/startup, medium, large) and job function (e.g., sales, strategy, operations, finance) were particularly important factors. For example, in a large company, any role I took would probably be more specialized and narrowly focused. That situation is totally different than working in a small company or startup where there is plenty of work to be done, but not enough hands, meaning that you may find yourself handling many different types of projects.

After building out the different financial and nonfinancial job function possibilities, I identified at least three sample companies for each category by running online

(continued)

(*continued*)

searches (e.g., "top investment banks in NYC," "top startups in NYC"), reading industry and career guides (e.g., Vault Guides), and reviewing company ranking lists (e.g., Fortune 100 Best Companies to Work For, 100 Best Places to Work In NYC, Crain's List of Best Places to Work In NYC). I limited my search to companies with offices in New York City, because I knew I wanted to stay there.

Step 2: Explore Through Networking

While you can learn a great deal through the World Wide Web, it can only take you so far. Networking and setting up informational interviews with those in your network can help you get the "real story" about potential roles and companies.

Informational Interviews with Current Connections

Think of an informational interview as an opportunity to catch up with a friend or learn more about an acquaintance, where you're trying to better understand their experience and perspective with a role and/or company that you could be interested in. Informational interviews may be able to answer the following questions for you.

Roles

- What is it really like to work in this role? Can you walk me through a typical day? Do you like what you do?
- Is there room for growth in this role or on the team? What's the typical tenure of people on this team and what do they do after leaving the team? Is it relatively easy for people in this role to transition to other roles in the company?

- What type of person would do well in this role? Are you looking for someone with a particular skill set?
- Given my interests and skills, do you think I'd be a good fit for this role or some other role within the company?

Companies

- What is it like to work at this company? Do people generally feel excited about working for the company?
- Is a typical workload and day similar across teams in the company? Are there generally expectations for night and weekend work? If so, how does that usually come about?
- Does the company allow employees the flexibility to work remotely either occasionally or full-time?
- How are the employee benefits (e.g., 401(k), health benefits)?
- What do you like most about working for this company?
- What don't you like as much about working for this company?

I recommend you start the networking process by reviewing your current contacts on LinkedIn, Facebook, and any other social media or networking site you use. Be on the lookout for connections that are working in a company or role that you are interested in learning more about. Once you've identified a list of contacts, reach out to those people to set up phone calls, coffee meetings, or lunches.

When reaching out, be specific with your ask so the connection can evaluate if they can help you and so they understand the time commitment required. Keep in mind that your ask should *not* be for a job unless you know the person very well. If speaking on the phone or meeting in person, be respectful of the person's time by being prompt and not taking up more than the scheduled time.

If you meet a connection for coffee or lunch, offer to pay for them – they are doing you a favor by meeting. Follow up after your discussion to thank the person for their time, state that you'll keep them posted on your progress, and offer to be a resource.

Build New Connections

What if you only have a couple of years of work experience and don't have many connections or have already "networked" with your direct connections? On LinkedIn, work with your direct connections to get an introduction to relevant people *they're* connected to. Research and attend events that may be interesting to you through meetup.com, your alumni association, or volunteering activities.

Augustine says, "Don't assume networking has to be only with your co-workers or fellow alumni. In fact, meeting people through your hobbies could be an effective way to casually approach networking, as well as an alternative to more structured events. As you network, be mindful that the two most important types of people to connect with are those who are in your desired industry and the social butterflies with vast networks."

Networking Done Right

Sometimes, networking can feel icky, transactional, and self-serving, but it doesn't have to be that way if you recast what your goal is. In particular, I think that people are the most successful at networking when they perceive it as an opportunity to meet, learn from, and potentially help new people. With that in mind, consider these pointers to help you maximize the time and energy (and yes, money) you invest in networking.

Network All the Time (Not Only When You Need Something)

"To be successful and understand what's possible, you need to proactively reach out to people whom you don't work with on a daily basis. Without those key contacts, it's easy to become isolated in a situation where the very people who can help you get ahead – and who you can be the most helpful to – have no idea how good you are, what your true interests are, or, for that matter, that you even exist."

Fran Hauser, former President of Digital at Time, Inc. and author of *The Myth of the Nice Girl*

Prepare

"Determine your goals: Ask yourself what you are looking for from the relationships you hope to develop. Are you anticipating making contacts with a specific future employer? Meeting a new mentor who can provide career guidance or industry expertise? Meeting new people in your industry? Intentionally identifying your networking goals will help you structure the questions you want to ask, prepare your elevator pitch, and determine requests you have for your contacts."

Paul Wolfe, Senior Vice President of Human Resources at Indeed

Learn, Listen, and Find Shared Interests

"Instead of approaching networking like a nonpersonal business transaction, we should all practice what I like to call organic networking. 'Organic networking' is when your only goal is to better understand that person's experience and place in the world. This agenda-less approach is much more natural and you end up learning a lot more about the person. Approach all conversations as an opportunity

(continued)

(*continued*)

to learn, rather than teach. Always remember to practice active listening, too. You'll be surprised at how natural and easy the conversation is when you think of networking in this mindset."

Richard Moross, CEO and Founder at MOO

Offer Help

"The best tip to build your network is to add value first. Do it before you try to make an ask or take value from someone you just met. An easy way to add value is to send someone an event or article they might be interested in with a short, personalized message. You could also host a simple gathering (like a cocktail party) to connect people in your town. Over time, as you build your network and develop a reputation as someone who offers value, your rewards will come."

Nick Gray, Founder at Museum Hack

Follow Up

"The most important – and often missed – skill when networking, is what happens after any interaction. How many tattered business cards have you fished out of the bottom of your briefcase or laundry? The real work is being meticulous around capturing all the notes (even the small talk), prioritizing your relationships, and following through on anything you discussed or promised. Simple to understand, but hard to implement."

Zvi Band, CEO and Co-Founder at Contactually

Clarify Your Value to People

"Always give that person a specific reason that you are a great fit or a worthy contact. If you aren't going to invest in the personal message and positioning, then you aren't worthy of a response. Keep it short and specific, and show that you really understand the role of the person that you are seeking to connect with."

Antonia Hock, Vice President at the Ritz-Carlton Leadership Center

Step 3: Narrow Down Possible Roles

While you may have listed numerous possible roles, companies, and industries at the beginning of the chapter, through online research and informational interviews, you should have been able to slowly eliminate some options. Even so, you may be left with a number of roles to choose from. As discussed earlier, your goal is to ultimately narrow your search to one type of position, and two at most (and hopefully roles that are somewhat related). This will make it easier to market yourself and for prospective employers to understand your story.

Imagine the alternative. If you embarked on a job search for sales roles, computer programming positions, and writing gigs, how would you position your one LinkedIn profile? Think about how different each of your resumes would have to be and the amount of time it would take to change your elevator pitch and frame of mind for each role. What if you were interviewing for a computer programmer role and a sales role in the same day? It's exhausting to even think about that!

What Do I Mean by One Type of Role?

When I say to narrow down your search to one or two types of positions, I don't want you to think you have to overly restrict yourself. For example, if you are interested in marketing, your one role type doesn't have to be as specific as saying, "I want to be a brand manager for a consumer packaged goods company." Instead, your one target role could be a marketing role that allows you to directly or indirectly help brands sell their products, while utilizing your strategy and analytical skills. That way, you're not limited to just a narrow set of companies. With the broader target, you could work at a company, like Procter & Gamble, to help market a specific product, such as Tide. Or you could work at a company that helps brands market their products, like an advertising agency. This strategy allows you to narrow your search sufficiently such that you can use the same marketing message across roles. At the same time, it keeps your search broad enough to maximize your potential opportunities.

Two Questions for Small Transitions

If your goal is to transition to a role that is related to what you're doing today, Paul Wolfe, Senior Vice President of Human Resources at Indeed, suggests evaluating each potential role and asking yourself: 1) Are you qualified to do the job? and 2) Do you actually want to do this job?[2]

Take some time to ask yourself these questions for your list of remaining roles. Cross off any roles where your answers aren't "yes" for each question. If you don't feel you have enough information to answer these questions for a particular role, set up more informational interviews to gather the data you need to make a decision.

Considerations for Larger Changes

If you're targeting roles you may not be qualified to do today, track down the answers to the following questions to narrow down your paths to pursue.

Money and Time Required

- What skills and experience do you need to gain to meet the minimum requirements of your target role?

- How long will it take you to gain the needed requirements, and how much will it cost? Are you willing to devote the time and money to gain the necessary experience?
- If you are able to make the intended change, would you need to take a pay cut from your current salary? If so, have you built up the financial runway needed to make this path feasible? Would you have the emotional support of loved ones to make this type of move?

Competitive Advantages
- Do you have any valuable skills that may be transferable to the target role?
- Do you have any unique connections that could help you get your foot in the door or decrease the transition time?
- Have former colleagues or others in positions similar to you (at your company or competitors) been able to transition to this type of role?

What's It Going to Be?

Of your possible career roles that remain, narrow them down to one or two. Once you've narrowed down your paths, fill in Table 9.1 (also available at www.workyourmoneybook.com):

- **Prioritization**: Order your top one or two roles by inputting your top choice into the Role #1 column and your second choice into the Role #2 column.
- **New Skills Required**: If you don't currently meet all of the skill and experience requirements, list the skills you'll need to build to make yourself a competitive candidate.
- **Time Needed**: List out how much time it may take to build up the new skills and experience.
- **Money Needed**: Estimate how much money it may take for any required training.
- **Small Ways to Test If You'd Like This Path**: You might be able to participate in events, activities, trainings, or volunteer opportunities to gather more data about whether you'd actually

Table 9.1   Prioritizing Potential Job Roles.

Prioritization	Role #1	Role #2
Role Name		
New Skills Required		
Time Needed		
Money Needed		
Small Ways to Test If You'd Like This Path		
What Does Success Look Like in Six Months?		
What Does Success Look Like in One Year?		

want to do this job for 40-plus hours a week. Put any ideas you have in this row.

- **What Does Success Look Like in Six Months?** Think about a realistic milestone for each path six months from now. What type of result would you be happy with? For a small transition, you may say that you'd like to have secured a new job in six months. For a larger transition, you may put down that you hope to have completed a particular training to fill any skills gap that may exist.
- **What Does Success Look Like in One Year?** Similar to the above, what would success look like for each path in one year from now?

Step 4: Close the Skills Gap

Now that you've narrowed down your roles to pursue one or two, you can start looking into how to gain new skills and experiences, if needed. The good news is, it's become much easier to learn new skills outside of an advanced degree program, making it faster and cheaper for you. But the learning is only half the battle. Augustine says, "It's also important to be able to highlight *how* you've been able to apply new skills. One of the easiest ways to do so outside of your current workplace is through skills-based volunteering, either with a nonprofit organization that interests you or through your school's alumni association."

Option 1: Learning Opportunities Through Your Current Company

One of the most efficient ways to gain new skills may be right underneath your nose – that is, leveraging resources offered by your current employer. You can access learning and training opportunities at your current job through:

- **Classes and Webinars**: Some companies offer on-demand and/or live classes on a variety of topics, including Excel, PowerPoint, data analysis, writing, or even coding. Other companies may fully or partially subsidize the cost of taking outside courses, particularly if you can create a business case for why the courses may increase your effectiveness in your current role.
- **Projects on Your Team**: Consider whether you may be able to take on projects in your current role that could help you build needed skills for a new job. Are there any gaps on the team that you could fill in, or projects you can take on that would allow you to build new skills and make your manager's life easier?
- **Projects Outside Your Team**: You might also be able to build needed skills by assisting another team at your company on an assignment. Such projects can also allow you to expand your network and increase your visibility. In the process, you may be able to position yourself for a more ideal role within your current company.

Option 2: Learning Opportunities Outside Your Company

With a little research and creativity, you can also find opportunities outside of your company to build job skills. In particular, you can receive academic and on-the-ground training through:

- **Individual Classes**: Online and offline courses can enable you to build the skills you need for a role or industry in a short period of time, and often at an affordable price. While these courses may not lead to a fancy Harvard MBA, you can *still* call them out on your resume. Course work signals to employers that you're a hard worker and a self-starter. Many institutions and universities also offer professional certifications in specialized fields, which can help give you a competitive edge. You can find class opportunities through a number of resources, including General Assembly, Khan Academy, Udemy, Coursea, colleges and universities, and industry-specific associations and publications.

- **Volunteering**: You may be able to build new skills and gain hands-on work experience *for free* by volunteering at a nonprofit or community organization. For example, if you wanted to develop your marketing skills, you could offer to provide free consulting services to a local charity for a couple of hours a week. Volunteering might also allow you to connect with and learn from others who have more experience in your desired field. Sites like Catchafire, VolunteerMatch, All for Good, and Create the Good can help you find available opportunities.
- **Advanced Degree Program**: Enrolling in a graduate program could make sense in certain situations. Some fields, such as law, medicine, and teaching, require advanced degrees. If a graduate degree isn't mandatory to transition to your target role or career, be absolutely clear on what you want to gain from graduate school that you can't get elsewhere. Be sure to weigh the benefits and costs, including the required time commitment to both apply for and attend school. You might also consider "test driving" graduate school by enrolling in an online or in-person course related to your prospective degree.

Ready, Set, Go!

Having narrowed down your possible job roles to one or two and begun gaining new skills and experiences, you've done a lot of the hard preparation needed to run a successful job search. In the next chapter, you'll leverage a lot of what you did in this chapter to identify, apply, and secure job opportunities.

Chapter 10

Take Action to Change Your Job

With a solid game plan in place, a lot of the hard work that changing your job requires is behind you. Now it's all about execution, which entails finding and applying for roles, positioning yourself effectively, interviewing, and evaluating offers.

But first, a word of warning: even after strategically narrowing your focus to one or two paths, a career change often requires a great deal of patience. According to an October 2018 survey by Randstad US, job seekers take five months on average to find a new role – and that's just the average.[1]

"There are many factors beyond your control that influence your job search timeline, including the state of the job market, industry developments, and luck," says Amanda Augustine, career expert at TopResume. "The good news is, there are numerous strategies for positioning yourself as a more qualified candidate, while potentially decreasing your job search timeline."

In this chapter, you'll learn about a number of tried-and-true strategies that can help you search for a job as effectively and efficiently as possible, without sacrificing the career priorities that you've identified. Feeling pumped yet? Let's dive right in.

Identify and Apply for Opportunities

There are three main ways to identify job opportunities that align with your interests and skills: by submitting job applications, engaging with recruiters, and networking. Because no single job-hunting strategy works best for every situation, I encourage you to use all of them for the first three months, observe which strategies are most effective for you, and then tweak your job search activities accordingly.

Let's take a moment now to review each of these job search techniques, including the potential pros and cons.

Submit Job Applications

You can easily jumpstart your job hunt by searching and applying for publicly available job postings online. This approach is especially effective if you are seeking roles that squarely match your skills and prior experience.

While applying to jobs online is as simple as the click of a button, actually receiving a response may prove more difficult. Glassdoor found that the average job posting attracts 250 applications, with just four to six people receiving an interview, and one person being offered the job.[2] Because of these challenging odds, Augustine recommends applying for at least five jobs a week that seem like potential fits. You should tailor your application and resume for each position, incorporating key terms from the job description to get past automated applicant tracking systems. We'll discuss exactly how to do this later in this chapter.

Engage with Recruiters

Third-party recruiters can be a valuable resource when seeking a new role because they are often able to connect you directly with employers, while also sharing industry insights and career search tips that make you a more informed and competitive candidate. Job hunters who are seeking roles at the executive level or within a specific industry may find recruiters to be especially helpful. When testing out the recruiter route, Augustine recommends contacting three to five new recruiters a week who fill positions in your target industry or job function.

Network

Networking can be the most effective strategy of all because you may be able to discover opportunities that have not been made publicly available (otherwise known as "the hidden job market"), while also potentially allowing you to bypass automated resume filters. In fact, Blair Decembrele, Director of Global Marketing Communications and Career Expert at LinkedIn, says job applicants who are referred by an employee are nine times more likely to get hired.

While networking can get you terrific results, this strategy does require patience and perseverance. In particular, networking is most successful when you do it regularly. That's why Augustine recommends that you block off time throughout the week to focus on networking activities such as attending industry events and connecting or reconnecting with people who work in a role or at a company that interests you. The networking process can also come at a financial cost that you may need to factor into your budget.

Position Yourself Effectively

In his book *The Lean Startup*, author Eric Ries says instead of marketing yourself to millions, sell yourself to one.[3] While the advice is intended for entrepreneurs, I think that job hunters can also learn a lot from Ries's words.

In particular, you can improve your hiring pitch by clearly articulating why you are a competitive candidate, and customizing your resume for each job.

Make It Clear

When developing your resume, try to make it as easy as possible for the hiring manager or recruiter to understand how your experience, qualifications, and job goals make you a good fit for a particular position. In other words, connect the dots for your prospective employer rather than have them try to guess the who, what, where, when, and why. This is especially important if you are looking to change industries.

When I was looking to transition industries, one of the big mistakes I made was failing to present my resume in an understandable way that would resonate with prospective employers. Below are actual examples of the bullets I used on my resume to describe some of my day-to-day responsibilities in finance:

- *Analyze all loan stratifications and balance sheets used for transactions. Lead collateral and structuring teams in performing cashflow, residual, borrow benefit, prepay, and cohort default analyses to optimize deal structuring.*
- *Structure and execute risk management solutions utilizing European/Bermudan swaptions, cancelable swaps, and various interest rate swaps, including fixed payer swaps, basis swaps, and constant maturity swaps.*

Does that read like a foreign language to you? It might as well have been.

Especially because I was looking to switch industries, my job search campaign would have been much more effective if I lost the confusing jargon and described my responsibilities in everyday terms that employers outside of investment banking could understand. But simplification is not enough. It's important to make sure a prospective employer not only understands *what* you did, but also *why* it should matter to them.

You will discover several benefits by simplifying and aligning your job responsibilities with those of the role you're seeking when writing your resume. First, a broader audience, including automated resume filters, will be able to understand what your work has entailed. You may also be able to uncover valuable skills and experiences that you hadn't identified before. In my own case, when I was targeting roles in nonfinancial organizations, I often came across job descriptions that cited project management experience as a desired qualification. Initially, I'd feel demoralized. "Damn it," I would think to myself. "I'm not a project manager. None of the experience on my resume matches what this company wants." But later on in my search, after I had revised my resume to simplify my experiences, I came to realize that many of the tasks I had handled while executing financial transactions were actually forms of project management. The truth was, I had more transferable skills than I thought I did – all I needed to do was dig a little deeper.

Make It Custom

If you've ever had a piece of clothing customized just for you, you know how much better it feels than a mass-produced item from off the store rack. The custom clothing may cost more money and take more time to get, but as a result, you receive a perfect fit. You could think of resumes in a similar way. Tailoring your resume for each job posting may take more time, but it could increase your chances of receiving a positive response from an employer.

According to research from Ladders, recruiters spend an average of six seconds before making a decision on whether a candidate is a fit for a role.[4] And that's if your resume even gets seen by a human. Data from Jobscan suggests that 98% of the Fortune 500 companies use applicant tracking systems to weed out unqualified candidates and manage the recruitment process.[5] These technologies identify and prioritize candidates by finding resumes that match keywords and qualifications in the job description.

This is why it's important not only to create a customized resume for each *career path* you are considering but also for each *role* you are pursuing. To do so, I recommend the following two-part approach:

- **Base Resumes**: Develop a customized base resume for each of your potential career paths, which you can use as a starting point for any individual job applications. You should have, at most, two potential career paths!
- **What to Customize**:
  - **Responsibilities and Skills**: Based on each job's description and requirements, determine the most relevant responsibilities and skills to highlight on your resume, and consider omitting less applicable responsibilities.
  - **Keywords**: Compare the keywords used in a job description with the language in your resume. If the job description and your resume are describing the same activity, but in different ways, look to incorporate some of the jargon and keywords that are in the job description. In this way, you will be able to translate your past experiences into words the system and hiring team can understand. (Of course, do not invent skills or experience in order to match the job description. That would be lying!)

Interview Tips

As you're identifying and applying for jobs, you may begin to get interview invites, which is a promising sign! To make the most of these opportunities, there is a fair amount of preparation that you can do before each interview to set yourself up for success.

Research, Research, Research

Doing your research on the company, industry, and role will ensure you come off as genuinely interested in the opportunity, help you anticipate potential questions, and prepare you to talk intelligently about the industry and marketplace dynamics.

I encourage you to use the following questions as a guide for where to focus your research:

Industry

- What is the current state of the industry?
- Have there been recurring themes in the news about the industry?

Company

- Within the industry, where does the company fit in, and what is its reputation?
- What has been going well for the company?
- What are some challenges the company is dealing with?
- Do people generally like working for the company?

Team

- How many people work on the team?
- How is the team structured in terms of roles and responsibilities?
- Are the team's key stakeholders internal or external?
- Do members of the team typically stay on the team for a long time or is there frequent turnover?

Role

- How long has the role been available? If it's been available for a long time, why has the company had a hard time filling it?
- How does the role fit into the larger team and company?
- What is the approximate all-in salary of the role or similar roles? How is this broken down between base salary, bonus, and equity?

Interviewers

- How many people will you be meeting with?
- Are the interviewers all on the hiring team?

- How long have each of the interviewers been at the company and on the team? What were their past experiences? What personal interests do they have?

Have Solid Answers for "Why?" Questions

"Why?" questions – which explore your motivations for seeking a role – are often asked of prospective candidates, especially those looking to make large changes in their careers. They are also good questions for you to know the answer to so that you can determine how attractive the particular role is to you.

Common "why?" questions to prepare for include:

- Why do you want to work at this company?
- Why do you want to work on this team?
- Why would you be a good fit for this role?
- Why is now the right time for you to make a change?

Come Prepared with Questions for Interviewers

Nothing frustrates an employer more in an interview situation than when a potential hire answers all of the questions successfully, but fails to ask any questions of their own. Interviews should be a two-way street, providing both the employer and the candidate an opportunity to assess whether they would be well-matched based on their respective preferences and priorities. Asking questions and digging for more information helps give you clues on what the job may be like, so that if you do receive an offer, you will be more likely to succeed in the job. Coming prepared with questions also signals to interviewers that you are actually interested in the role, and would likely accept the position if it were offered to you.

Some common questions that you could ask in an interview include:

- What does a typical day look like for you?
- What do you like most about the job?

- Why did you originally join this team?
- What has made you stay on the team?
- What is the biggest challenge the team is facing now? Is it an industry development, a competitor, or something else?
- How would you describe the manager's management style?

You should build off of these standard questions with individualized questions that reflect your own priorities and concerns. If you find yourself struggling to come up with questions for a particular interview, revisit your answers to the "why?" questions we discussed earlier. Depending on your responses, you may realize the role *isn't* interesting to you, after all. If so, I still encourage you to attend the interview so that you can practice your skills and potentially gain competitive research – both of which will help you when the right opportunity does come along.

Practice!

As a child, I played the piano, and my parents had this dream of me someday playing in Carnegie Hall in New York City, which I somehow actually did. While I was at Carnegie Hall, I stopped by the gift shop and remember seeing a T-shirt that read, "How do you get to Carnegie Hall? Practice, practice, practice."

That's true not only of piano but also of any other activity, including interviewing – any skill requires practice and experience, above all else.

That being said, I am the first to acknowledge that preparing for an interview can feel overwhelming, especially if you haven't been in an interview in a while. As a first step, I recommend writing out the key messages you want to convey in bullet form. For example, "I'm looking to work in a more specialized role that would build on my interest in [xyz]," or "My experience demonstrates that I have a unique knack for [fill-in-the-blank]." After jotting down the big-picture messages you want to cover, think of ways to slip them into an interview in response to questions you'll likely be asked.

Then run through the set of questions and answers three or four times, reciting your responses aloud.

I've found that each time I run through my answers, I notice either points I may be forgetting or areas in my answers where I may be stumbling. When this happens, I go back to my written answers to tweak the messages I want to relay. Finally, if possible, I practice these question-and-answer exchanges with a friend or family member, and solicit their feedback on how I could improve the content and my body language.

Right now, I bet you're thinking that this process sounds a lot like memorization, and that you may not want to use this technique because you may come off as robotic in the interview. I totally see your point. The truth is, there's a fine line between the technique that I'm proposing and rote memorization. But you can work around that. Specifically, I recommend you practice delivering your responses using different wording. Your goal should be to convey the general idea, rather than to repeat your written messaging points verbatim. That way, depending on the interviewer's style, you can change the tone of your answers to help establish more of a rapport with the other person and respond more naturally.

Evaluate Opportunities

When at last you do receive a job offer, you may be tempted to seal the deal as soon as possible. Understandably! Being wanted feels good, especially if you are frustrated with your current job situation. But make sure to thoroughly evaluate any potential role and opportunity before making the leap.

You can leverage the framework you used to evaluate your current job in Chapter 3 to also analyze your potential job. While you won't have nearly as much data as you do for your current role, you should be able to rely on your research, informal conversations, and interviews to perform a directional analysis.

One strategy that I've found particularly helpful is to create a side-by-side comparison of my current job analysis, versus

Table 10.1   Current Job Factor Analysis.

Work Factor	Translation	Obstacles to Improving Job Factor
1. Are You Getting Value?	Do you like what you do on a day-to-day basis?	
2. Are You Adding Value?	Do you feel you're able to make an impact in your job?	
3. Are You Increasing Your Value in the Market?	Does your current role expand or decrease your future job options?	
4. Does Your Role Align with Your Values?	Do your office environment, work schedule flexibility, and employee benefits improve your overall quality of life?	
5. Do You Feel Valued?	Do you feel like you are being fairly rewarded through pay, promotions, and work responsibilities?	

the potential job analysis. You can use Tables 10.1 and 10.2 as a starting point (also available at www.workyourmoneybook .com), but feel free to add details and bullet points to give yourself additional context, including pros and cons around each job factor.

Job Comparison Analysis

These additional questions may further help to inform your decision:

- What requirements must the potential job meet in order for it to be "better" than my current job, and closer to my ideal job? For example, what outcomes have to occur, and how likely or unlikely are those outcomes?

Table 10.2 Potential Job Factor Analysis.

Work Factor	Translation	Potential Considerations and Obstacles
1. Are You Getting Value?	Do you think you would like what you did on a day-to-day basis?	
2. Are You Adding Value?	Do you feel you would be able to make an impact in the job?	
3. Are You Increasing Your Value in the Market?	Would this job expand or decrease your future job options?	
4. Does Your Role Align with Your Values?	Do you think the office environment, work schedule flexibility, and employee benefits would improve your overall quality of life?	
5. Do You Feel Valued?	Do you feel you would be fairly rewarded through pay, promotions, and work responsibilities?	

- If I take this job and perform well, what type of role would I progress to after one or two promotions? What are the daily demands and sacrifices required of those jobs, and would I be willing to make those trade-offs?
- Consider the worst-case scenario: What if I accept this job, and everything goes wrong? Where would that leave me, and would I be able to deal with it? What's the best-case scenario?

This analysis should give you a framework for how to evaluate an opportunity. With that said, of course you will never have 100% perfect information, and that's okay. At some point, you have to make an educated decision based on the information you have at the time, and move forward.

Rinse and Repeat

Even if you've put a lot of thought and care into your job plan, you will likely run into roadblocks at some point or another. Personally, I found the job search process to be iterative: first, you form a hypothesis about what you think may be a good path; then you test your hunch by researching, networking, and taking on new projects.

As you progress through the steps outlined in this chapter, you'll accumulate more data and either continue proceeding on your way or change courses. You could very well start down one path, only to realize you dislike or lack the qualifications for the type of work you were pursuing. Or perhaps the dynamics in your current job shift during the course of your search so that your quality of life improves, causing you to rethink a career change.

The point is, you should be prepared to modify your initial job plan as you delve into the action items we've covered. In fact, you'll move closer to work you enjoy if you periodically take time to reflect on what's going well, what's not going well, and what needs to change.

Part IV

Optimize Your Finances

"The goal isn't to beat the market, prove how clever we are, or become the wealthiest family in town. Rather, the goal is to have enough to lead the life we want."

– Jonathan Clements

Most of us don't get interested in financial planning until we have a particular goal we want to achieve (why would we?). These goals typically center around major life events, like buying a home, funding a child's education, or saving for retirement. But why aren't we also considering our *career-related* goals more often – especially given how important it is to enjoy our jobs? In this section, you'll address that very question by crafting a comprehensive and viable financial plan that facilitates your desired career path.

Similar to how we approached your job strategy, you'll start by reflecting on your financial needs and priorities (which likely include some of those big-ticket items I mentioned earlier, in addition to your career objectives). You'll then make those goals specific to your individual situation by defining when you want to achieve each goal, estimating the monthly savings required, and prioritizing, revising, and eliminating goals as necessary to create a workable financial plan.

Once you know where you want to go financially, you'll be ready for everyone's favorite personal finance topic: investing. This chapter will outline no-frills strategies for how to invest wisely based on the goals you've set and your personal risk tolerance. Importantly, you'll also learn how to maintain your portfolio so that it successfully serves you for the long haul. And don't worry: we'll stick with simple concepts and cut out the confusing finance jargon that might have intimidated you out of investing in the past.

Last but not least, you'll be learning how to *protect* the money you've worked so hard to accrue through insurance and estate planning strategies. You'll come away with a better understanding of how to pick a health insurance policy, which additional types of insurance might make sense for you to purchase, and how to ensure that your estate is in good standing for the benefit of your loved ones. (And to all my millennial readers, I'm sorry to be the bearer of bad news, but you are *not* too young to at least start thinking about estate planning!)

Be sure to go to www.workyourmoneybook.com to access helpful templates related to exercises in this section. Now for the fun stuff: let's talk money, shall we?

Chapter 11

Chart Your Goals and How Much They Will Cost

"Is now a good time to buy a home?"

I receive this question like clockwork in nearly every personal finance speaking engagement I lead. And every time, I answer that rather than try to time the market (which is extremely difficult to do), you should make sure a home purchase aligns with your personal timeline and needs.

This advice applies to a broad range of financial goals. When we don't take the time to clearly define our values and objectives, we are prone to chasing the shiny object – whether it's the type of work we think we're "supposed" to do, or the financial goal we think we "should" achieve – rather than making decisions that are truly right for us.

In this chapter, you'll create a roadmap that is specific to your individual financial needs and wants. First, you'll consider your priorities to identify a number of different financial goals, much like you did in the beginning of Part 3, when you identified what a "good" job was for you. As you delve deeper, you'll make your goals more concrete by developing a timetable and quantifying the cost of each goal. Based on your savings rate, salary trajectory, and desired lifestyle, your initial list of financial goals may not be attainable. That's okay! You'll further review your goals and prioritize, revise, or eliminate them, until you have a feasible set by the end of the chapter – providing you a clear path toward making your preferred life a reality.

Step 1: Choose Your Destination

Where do you want to go? Answering that question is the first step to developing financial goals for yourself.

Most people's financial goals focus on either building a more solid financial foundation (e.g., by paying off debt or saving for an emergency fund) or protecting their long-term financial stability (e.g., by saving for a down payment for a home or retirement). When I work with clients, I like to classify financial goals into two categories: those that are mandatory and those that are optional. As you read this section, write down your goals in both categories.

Mandatory Goals

While everyone's goals will differ based on their particular needs and wants, certain financial items are mandatory. You should list and prioritize the following goals, if you haven't achieved them yet:

- **Save for an emergency fund**: If you don't have three to six months of living expenses set aside in cash, then saving for an emergency fund should be on your list of goals. While three to six months is the recommended benchmark, you may want to save more. I've worked with clients who wanted as much as 12 months of living expenses set aside because that's the amount that gave them peace of mind. The amount you'll want to save will depend on how stable your job is, how regular your income is, and the amount of money that will make you feel comfortable on a daily basis. Generally, the less stable your job and income are, the more you'll want to save in an emergency fund.

- **Pay off high-cost debt**: If you don't pay off your credit card balance in full every month and have other high-cost debt outstanding (e.g., personal loans), then you should include eliminating this debt on your list of goals.
- **Save for retirement, financial independence, and/or general life flexibility**: Regardless of whether you think of this goal as retirement, financial independence, or just general life flexibility, setting aside money for these goals early and often allows you to build good habits, lower your spending rate, and benefit from the growth of your money for a longer time. If you work for a company, your employer may make contributions to your retirement account as well. You read that right: many employers will put money into your retirement account based on a percentage of what you contribute. That's kind of like getting an increase in your salary without even having to ask or negotiate. Talk about a no-brainer!

Optional Goals

Your optional financial goals will be dictated by your personal preferences. I like to group optional financial goals into several subcategories:

- **Professional and educational**: Goals that are career-related (e.g., start a business, start a side hustle), or that consist of improving your human capital (e.g., go to graduate school, take personal enrichment classes, join a networking organization). Be sure to refer back to the great work you did in Part 3 of the book to confirm your job goals, and the potential cost of those goals.
- **Medium-sized savings goals**: Goals that may take less than five years to achieve (e.g., buy a car, save for a wedding, save for a vacation, donate to charity, prepay mortgages and/or student loans).
- **Large savings goals**: Goals that make take five or more years to reach (e.g., buy a home, save for children's education).

Should I Save to Buy a Home?

Many of my financial planning clients tell me during our first meeting that they want to save for a home. Of course they do – home ownership is the American Dream, right? But the reality isn't that simple; in fact, renting could make more sense than buying depending on your situation. I ask my clients three questions to help them determine whether a home purchase should be among their financial goals.

- **Can you buy?** First and foremost, buying a home needs to be financially feasible. Upfront, you'll need enough savings to put down a sufficient down payment, pay closing costs, and still have money left over for an emergency fund. On an ongoing basis, your total housing payment (i.e., mortgage, homeowners insurance, homeowners association fees, and property taxes) should be less than 28% of your gross income, and if you have other debt, your total housing and debt payments should be less than 36% of your gross income. Your credit score matters as well; generally, the higher your credit score, the more likely you'll be able to secure a lower mortgage rate.

- **Should you buy?** Most real estate agents and financial planners (including myself) suggest that as a rule of thumb, you might be better off renting unless you think you'll be living in the same home for at least five to seven years. Your time frame matters because there are a fair number of "frictional costs" involved when buying and selling real estate. A longer time horizon gives you more of an opportunity to realize price appreciation on your home to offset any transactional costs. Think about your job security and your plans to change careers or pursue an advanced degree, which could have a big influence on your time horizon.

- **Do you want to buy?** Regardless of whether you can or should buy a home, you'll also want to consider the amount of savings required to fund a home purchase in relation to your other financial goals. Most of us have a limited cash flow and need to prioritize some goals over others. In step 3, you'll walk through an exercise to determine which goals are most important to you.

Step 2: Map Out Your Path

Once you've identified *what* you want, the next step is figuring out *when* you want to achieve your goals, and *how much* each goal will cost. Table 11.1 shows an example goal template that you can find and use at www.workyourmoneybook.com, or create your own for this exercise. Regardless, you'll want to identify the following:

- **Goals**: Label the goal you want to achieve, whether it's buying a home, saving for an emergency fund, or any other goal you listed in the prior section.
- **Total upfront cost**: Determine how much each goal will cost. For most goals, you should be able to estimate the cost based

Table 11.1   Financial Goal-Setting Template.

Goal Name	Goal # 1	Goal # 2	Goal # 3	Total
(1) Total Upfront Cost				
(2) Timetable (in months)				N/A
(3) Existing Savings for Goal				
(4) Savings Required per Month ([1–3] ÷ 2)				

on some online research. For longer-term goals, such as saving for a child's education or retirement, use online calculators that incorporate estimated investment returns and inflation to arrive at the total cost and required monthly savings.

- **Timetable (in months)**: Define *when* you want or need to achieve each goal.
- **Existing savings for goal**: If you've already started saving money toward your goal, write down the amount you've set aside.
- **Savings required per month**: Calculate how much you'll need to save each month to achieve each goal on your list. In order to do this, subtract the existing savings you've set aside for a goal from the total upfront cost of the goal and then divide your resulting figure by the number of months available to save for the goal. For example, if it's currently the beginning of December 2019, and you want to save $12,000 for a vacation by December 2020, you'll have about 12 months to achieve that goal – meaning, you will need to save $1,000 a month to be successful (assuming you have no existing savings set aside).

How to Calculate Savings for a Home Purchase

I recently worked with a young married couple who wanted to buy a 700-square-foot, one-bedroom apartment in Manhattan in the next five years. My clients, Mary and Carl, had been renting for the last eight years, while trying to build up enough savings for a down payment. The process we went through to determine the savings needed could apply to any market.

As a first step, we looked at apartment listings online so that they could get a sense of the types of properties they might be able to purchase in various price ranges. Right off the bat, Mary and Carl agreed that they would rather have more space than live in a "sexier" area – so they scratched off downtown Manhattan from their list of possible neighborhoods. They also concurred that having a doorman and elevator would be nice, but was not really necessary for their situation or lifestyle – so they eliminated buildings with these amenities. After considering a couple of other factors, they agreed to target a walk-up apartment in midtown or uptown Manhattan that in five years would cost approximately $500,000 based on current market averages, plus an estimated inflation rate of 2% per year.

Next, we ran some hard numbers, which you can review in Table 11.2. Carl and Mary wanted to aim to make a 20% down payment – or $100,000. For planning purposes, they assumed they'd also need to pay 6% in closing costs, or another $30,000. To calculate how much they had to save each month, we took the total cost of their goal ($130,000), and subtracted out any existing savings they had reserved for a home purchase. By renting, Carl and Mary had saved $30,000 toward a down payment, so they only needed to save $100,000 more. We then divided the remaining savings Carl and Mary needed ($100,000) by the number of months until they'd need the money (60 months), which came to $1,667.

Table 11.2   Required Savings for One-Bedroom Apartment.

Goal	Buy a One-Bedroom Apartment in Manhattan
(1) Total Upfront Cost	$130,000 ($100,000 down payment + $30,000 closing costs)
(2) Timetable (in months)	5 years (60 months)
(3) Existing Savings for Goal	$30,000
(4) Savings Required per Month ([1–3] ÷ 2)	$1,667

Step 3: Refine Your Plan

Once you've listed all of your goals and the cost of each goal, take a look at the total monthly savings needed to fund *all* of your goals over the next several years. Compare the monthly savings needed to fund your goals with your current monthly savings, which you calculated in Chapters 4 and 5. Is the total amount you need to save each month *much more* than you have available (and more than you may have available after a job change)? If so, don't panic – there are several strategies you can use to make the numbers work. Your options, from the least to most strenuous, include:

- Prioritize your goals.
- Change the timetable for your goals.
- Revise the cost of certain goals.
- Eliminate certain goals.
- Revisit your expenses.

Option 1: Prioritize Your Goals

At the beginning of this chapter, you had the opportunity to identify a number of financial goals with no real restrictions. Now, I want you to take a closer look at the goals you listed and categorize them into the following buckets:

- **Must-haves:** These are goals that you must accomplish to ensure your financial security – no ifs, ands, or buts. Your must-haves should include all of the applicable mandatory goals that we reviewed earlier, including saving for an emergency fund, paying off high-cost debt, and saving for retirement or financial independence. You may also choose to classify some other financial goals on your list as "must-haves" based on your personal values and needs. For example, job-related goals may fall into this bucket.
- **Nice-to-haves:** Nice-to-haves are financial goals that you could sacrifice without materially impacting your stability or happiness. These goals may include buying a house, buying a new car, saving for a vacation, and so on.

Once you've categorized your goals into must-haves and nice-to-haves, add up the monthly savings needed for each bucket. Do you have sufficient savings to set aside for all must-have goals, and some nice-to-have goals? If not, read on for more strategies you can use to make a workable plan!

Option 2: Change the Timetable for Your Goals

Initially, we assumed that you would start saving for all your financial goals today. However, you can alter the timing of some of your goals based on their level of priority to create a more workable plan. Let's say you had initially aspired to create an emergency fund, pay off credit card debt, and save for a house purchase within the next three years. If that wasn't a feasible plan, you could adjust your timing to save for your highest-priority goals (i.e., building an emergency fund and paying off credit card debt) within the next year. After achieving those goals, you could then divert all of your savings toward saving for a down payment.

Take my clients Corey and Hannah. When we started working together, they told me their main goals were to save for retirement, their child's education, and a home purchase. They estimated that they needed to save $3,000 a month to be able to fund their goals. The problem was, Corey and Hannah were only saving $2,000 a month. To bridge the gap, we discussed a variety of options. Switching to more-demanding, higher-paying jobs could fill the gap, but that didn't really align with their desired lifestyle or job interests. Neither did spending their limited free time pursuing side hustles to earn extra cash. We then walked through whether they could cut any other existing expenses based on the strategies discussed in Chapter 5, but we had already optimized their situation previously.

Given these restrictions, I worked with Corey and Hannah to tweak the timetable for their plan. They decided that their timeline for a home purchase was more flexible than that of their other goals. As a result, they agreed to focus on saving for college and retirement in the immediate term, and then begin putting money toward a down payment as their salaries increased.

Option 3: Revise the Cost of Certain Goals

Another effective strategy for creating a feasible financial plan is to amend the cost of your larger, nice-to-have goals, such as saving for a house, buying a car, and saving for a child's education. In the previous example, Mary and Carl had wanted to purchase a $500,000 home in five years, but let's say they can't get the numbers to work. By forgoing certain amenities, they might be able to instead target a $400,000 home, which would lower the upfront cost of their goal from $130,000 to $104,000.

A hot topic for many of my clients is saving for their child's college education. They may initially assume they need to fully fund the cost of a four-year, private university, but after taking into consideration their other goals, some decide to scale back and fund half the cost of a private college, or fully fund a public university instead.

Option 4: Eliminate Certain Goals

Joey Gladstone, a character on the '90s sitcom *Full House*, often got big laughs for using the catchphrase "Cut it out."[1] You might apply Joey's surprisingly wise words to some of your financial goals if your plan still isn't feasible after using the other strategies we've discussed.

For example, saving for a vacation home may have sounded like a great idea in the beginning of the chapter when you were letting your dreams run wild. But you might decide to throw that particular goal by the wayside after weighing a few weeks a year in Cancun against paying off your existing debt. This may be the iterative process you go through to determine if any goals are expendable.

Option 5: Revisit Your Expenses

When all is said and done, your goals may still cost more than you can save each month. If so, I encourage you to refer back to Chapters 4 and 5, which provide guidance for modeling out and cutting your expenses. Take a closer look at these costs, and identify which ones you may be able to decrease in favor of your financial goals.

Are We There Yet?

By developing a workable financial plan that includes your goals and a timetable for achieving them, you'll take the first step to align what you value with where you spend your money.

On a day-to-day basis, having a financial plan can help inform your decisions while also serving as a motivating force for you to save more money. As an added benefit, you'll be less likely to get distracted or experience FOMO (fear of missing out) by what other people are spending their money on.

With a workable set of goals, you're ready to dive into the world of investing. In the next chapter, we'll discuss how you can grow your money to achieve your goals and priorities.

Chapter 12
What You Need to Know About Investing

I used to have regular lunches with two of my co-workers who shared a lot of common interests with me (namely, old-school Nintendo games, Penguins hockey, and by-the-slice pizza joints). Usually we talked about these topics at length. But I remember one afternoon when the conversation turned to investing.

"Man, I've made so much money on energy stocks this year," one of my co-workers said.

"Yeah, energy has been doing so well. I've also got money in some leveraged ETFs, which I think will pay off big time," my other colleague boasted. Then he turned to me. "How about you, Roger – what are you investing in these days?"

I couldn't really contribute to this particular conversation; not only did I have a small investment portfolio at the time, but I couldn't remember what my few holdings were or why I had chosen them. I felt a little like Marty McFly in the movie *Back to the Future*, when he asks Doc Brown, "What the hell is a gigawatt?"[1] Except the question going through my head was, "What the hell is an ETF?" It seemed like everyone knew more about investing than I did and was somehow always able to pick winning investments. So instead of answering my co-worker, I mumbled some nonsense and then immediately changed the topic to what the best burger was in New York City.

Investing stressed the heck out of me for a long time, so I often tried to ignore its existence, although every now and then, I'd get motivated and try to self-study online. I'd read a couple of articles on CNBC and then head over to Bloomberg to plow through more. But afterward, I'd find myself more confused than before. Even on the rare occasions when I managed to understand the jargon-filled commentary, I didn't know how to apply what I read to my personal situation. Worst of all, I'd inevitably stumble across an article forecasting that the stock market was probably about to tank, so of course I'd get spooked into doing nothing and end up kicking the can down the road even further. The experience was particularly frustrating because I felt like I *should* be able to understand this investing stuff. I mean, I did work in finance after all!

I've come a long way since those days of baffled online research over a cold slice of Papa John's pizza. (I know, I know – I can't believe I ordered Papa John's in *New York City*, of all places.) What I understand now would have shocked me at the time, which is that investing doesn't have to be difficult! In fact, many financial experts and pundits try to overcomplicate investing either to sound smart, to scare you into depending on their services, or to mask the fact that they may not fully understand the concepts themselves.

In this chapter, I'll get right to the point by simplifying what you need to know about investing, why you need to know it, and how it applies to your personal situation, without the extraneous details and confusing lingo that has probably weighed you down in the past.

Why Investing Can Be Powerful

In Chapter 5, I covered how saving rather than investing can have a bigger impact on your bottom line early in your career. That doesn't mean it's not important to start investing early. While your investment returns won't make a huge difference in your quality of life when you have a smaller portfolio, saving and investing early helps you build good habits, and allows you to reap the benefits of compound interest for a longer period of time – meaning, earning money on top of the money you make from your original contributions.

Compound interest shows similarities with a snowball rolling down a hill. While the snowball may start small and grow modestly after the first couple of rolls, at some point, it'll gain momentum and significantly enlarge. The longer the hill, the more snow the snowball can accumulate. Similarly, the longer your money is invested, the more money you'll be able to earn. Even Albert Einstein was amazed by compound interest, calling it "the eighth wonder of the world."

As an example, say you put $5,000 into an investment account that earns an interest rate of 5% compounded annually, and then never deposit any additional money. As depicted in Table 12.1, after being invested for one year, your $5,000 investment earns $250 ($5,000 × 5%). In each subsequent year, your investment return isn't simply $250 – you earn 5% on your original investment of $5,000, as well as 5% on your investment earnings from all previous years (assuming you reinvest those earnings each year). This results in a modest incremental return of $13 more in your second year (5% of

Table 12.1 Comparing Earnings from Original Investment Versus Earnings on Earnings.

Year	Starting Balance	Investment Return on Initial Balance	Investment Return on Prior Investment Earnings	Ending Balance
1	$5,000	$250	$0	$5,250
2	$5,250	$250	$13	$5,513
3	$5,513	$250	$26	$5,788
4	$5,788	$250	$39	$6,078
5	$6,078	$250	$54	$6,381
10	$7,757	$250	$138	$8,144
15	$9,900	$250	$245	$10,395
20	$12,635	$250	$382	$13,266

Table 12.2 Months of Financial Runway built by Various Portfolios (Annually).

Portfolio Balance	Investment Return of 5%	Months of Financial Runway (for $100,000 of Living Expenses)
$5,000	$250	0.03
$50,000	$2,500	0.30
$500,000	**$25,000**	**3.00**
$5,000,000	$250,000	30.00

the previous year's investment return of $250), but after 15 years, your investment return on your prior investment earnings is nearly equivalent to the earnings from your initial investment!

While you may not get excited about earning $250 a year on $5,000, look at how your absolute investment return increases as your portfolio grows (see Table 12.2). When your portfolio reaches $500,000, a 5% return will kick off $25,000 a year – three months of financial runway for someone who spends $100,000 a year. That's a pretty good deal for not having to lift a finger or drag yourself into work. In other words, as your investment portfolio grows, it becomes that rich uncle you never had (or at least that's how I think about it).

Key Factors for Investing

Many different factors affect your investment return (read: how much money you make), with some having a larger impact than others. However, only a few of those factors are actually in your control.

- **Asset Allocation**: What you invest in
- **Asset Location**: Which type of accounts you put your investments in
- **Fees and Expenses**: How much you pay to invest

Let's review each of these factors to understand what they are, how they can impact your investment return, and how to think about what action you should take for your portfolio across these three factors.

What to Invest in (Asset Allocation)

The Basic Asset Types

While you may have stumbled across numerous investment types and vehicles, let's start by focusing on the three most common categories: cash, bonds, and stocks.

I'll start with cash because it's the easiest to understand and the asset you're probably most familiar with. Cash is simply money in a checking or savings account or another cash-like investment, like a certificate of deposit (CD) or money market fund.

Bonds Are Loans to a Company

Bonds are financial instruments used by companies to borrow money. If you buy a bond, you're essentially loaning money to a company. The financial benefit of investing in a bond is that you will receive interest payments on the loan amount. For example, let's say you loan $100 to Junebug Inc., which agrees to pay you $106 in one year. The extra $6 you receive, above and beyond your original $100 loan, represents the interest payment, or the financial benefit to you as the investor.

Stocks Are Partial Ownership in a Company

Stocks represent a partial ownership in a company. If you buy a stock, you can benefit financially by selling your shares for a profit down the line – assuming the stock price increases, of course.

In the meantime, stockholders are entitled to a portion of the company's assets and profits through dividends and stock buybacks. Dividends are payments made to shareholders from company profits. And a stock buyback is exactly what the name implies – a process through which the company repurchases existing shares of stock at the current price, decreasing the number of company shares overall. Stock buybacks increase the price for remaining shares because each share now represents a greater portion of the company's assets and profits. As a result, stockholders will earn a greater profit on their shares if they decide to sell them.

Companies decide whether to retain or distribute profits on a quarterly basis, and ask themselves: Would the shareholders benefit more if the remaining money were reinvested into the company (with the aim of further growing business earnings and therefore, the share price), or if they were to receive their share of the profits in the form of dividends or stock buybacks?

Mature companies, such as AT&T, may not have as many new or fast-growing projects to invest leftover profit in, so instead, they may return some money to shareholders in the form of dividends or share buybacks. On the other hand, fast-growing companies, like Facebook and Salesforce, may retain profits to further expand their businesses through internal projects and acquisitions.

Now I bet you're thinking: "Okay, smarty-pants. I can see that stock price growth and dividends both benefit investors. But let's get down to the brass tacks: if I decided to invest in the stock market, which benefit would make up the majority of my investment return?"

While the answer isn't so clear cut and will depend on your specific investment holdings, Table 12.3 demonstrates that for companies in the S&P 500 Index, the majority of returns for investors in these companies have historically come from an increase in stock prices, rather than from dividends.[2]

Taking a Closer Look at Risks versus Returns

Cash, bonds, and stocks each come with their own risks and potential returns. Generally, assets that have a wider range of possible

Table 12.3 Breakdown of S&P 500 Return Between Dividends and Capital Appreciation (Average Annualized Returns).

Time Period	Dividends	Capital Appreciation
1950–2017	3.4%	7.7%
2010–2017	2.2%	11.6%

Source: J.P. Morgan Asset Management.

returns from year to year are considered "riskier" than assets that have a narrower set of possible returns.

Cash, bonds, and stocks generally have the following risk and return characteristics:

- **Cash**: Least risky (lowest variation in returns), but provides lowest returns
- **Bonds**: Riskier than cash, but not as risky as stocks; generally returns more than cash, but less than stocks
- **Stocks**: Riskiest type of asset (highest variation in returns), but generally has the highest expected returns

To put some real numbers to this, refer to Table 12.4, which summarizes an analysis performed by Vanguard, showing the best, worst, and average annual returns for various mixes of stocks and bonds using indices that attempted to represent the broader stock and bond markets.

Table 12.4 Investment Returns for Different Mixes of Stocks and Bonds (1926–2018).[3]

Mix of Stocks and Bonds	Highest 1-Year Return	Lowest 1-Year Return	Average Annual Return
Stocks: 100% | Bonds: 0%	54%	−43%	10.1%
Stocks: 80% | Bonds: 20%	45%	−35%	9.4%
Stocks: 50% | Bonds: 50%	32%	−23%	8.2%
Stocks: 20% | Bonds: 80%	30%	−10%	6.6%
Stocks: 0% | Bonds: 100%	33%	−8%	5.3%

Source: Adapted from Vanguard; highest and lowest returns rounded to nearest whole percentage.

Let's take a closer look at the 100% stock portfolio (first row of Table 12.4). Over the time period of the analysis from 1926 to 2018, you'll notice that this portfolio earned the highest return in a single year at 54%, but it also had the greatest loss in a single year at −43%! That being said, over the long run, this all-stock portfolio brought in the highest average annual return, at more than 10%.

Now refocus your attention to the 100% bond portfolio (last row of Table 12.4). This portfolio produced the lowest average annual return of all of the portfolios (5.3%) over the time period analyzed, but it also lost the least amount of money in a single year (−8%).

What does this all mean? *Generally, as you increase the percentage of stocks in your investment portfolio, you may experience more variability in your returns from year to year.*

Let's put this concept into real-life terms. Say you had $100,000 to invest in any types of assets you wished. If you invested all that money into stocks, you could very well end up with $154,000 in a year from now (54% return); however, you could also be left with just $57,000 (−43% return). On the other hand, if you invested all that money into bonds, you may come away with $133,000 by year-end in the rosiest scenario (33% return); or you may lose $8,000 and be left with $92,000 in the worst-case scenario (−8% return).

Interestingly, though, these results change when we begin to look at different holding periods (i.e., the amount of time you own a stock or bond). In a 2018 study, J.P. Morgan Asset Management analyzed average annual returns of stocks and bonds over 1-, 5-, 10-, and 20-year holding periods.[4] The study's findings are depicted in Table 12.5.

Let's focus our attention on the 100% stock portfolio first (top of the table). You'll notice that while the returns for this portfolio ranged dramatically during one-year holding periods (similar to the Vanguard analysis), the amount of variability decreased dramatically for longer holding periods – and in the investor's favor. Specifically, if you look at the 5-year and 10-year portions of the table, you'll see that the all-stock portfolio returned, on average, as much as 20% to 30% annually, while in some periods, only lost 1% to 3% per year, on average. Finally, when you look at the portion of the table for

Table 12.5   Investment Returns for Different Holding Periods (1950–2017).

Mix of Stocks and Bonds	Highest Average Annual Return	Lowest Average Annual Return
Stocks: 100% | Bonds: 0%		
1-Year Holding Period	47%	−39%
5-Year Holding Period	28%	−3%
10-Year Holding Period	19%	−1%
20-Year Holding Period	17%	7%
Stocks: 50% | Bonds: 50%		
1-Year Holding Period	33%	−15%
5-Year Holding Period	21%	1%
10-Year Holding Period	16%	2%
20-Year Holding Period	14%	5%
Stocks: 0% | Bonds: 100%		
1-Year Holding Period	43%	−8%
5-Year Holding Period	23%	−2%
10-Year Holding Period	16%	1%
20-Year Holding Period	12%	1%

Source: Adapted from J.P. Morgan Asset Management.

the 20-year holding period, you'll find that negative average annual returns were eliminated entirely for all-stock portfolios – with the lowest average annual return at 7%, and the highest average annual return yielding 17%!

The takeaway is, stocks aren't bad or scary. While stocks could yield a wide range of positive or negative returns from year to year, the variability of your average annual return tends to decrease as you increase your holding period – and much of the downside of investing in stocks, from an average annual return perspective, could be minimized for longer holding periods. (Note: you'll still be subject to highs and lows along the way.)

Individual Holdings versus Diversified Portfolio

All right, let's recap what we've discussed so far: bonds are loans to a company, and stocks equate to ownership in a company. Stocks have much larger swings in investment returns than bonds from year to year, but over a long period of time, stocks generally produce a higher average return than bonds.

Now that you've got the basics down, should you just go out and start picking some individual stocks and bonds to fill your portfolio based on what you read online? My answer would be no, for a couple of reasons.

Less Diversification = Bigger Swings; More Diversification = Smaller Swings

Let's refer back to the Vanguard study on the variability of returns for different stock and bond portfolios that was summarized in Table 12.4. This study assumed you held a well-diversified portfolio consisting of hundreds of different companies' stocks and bonds, not just a stock and bond from a single company. If the table illustrated a portfolio consisting of a stock and bond from a single company, the swings in returns might have been much greater across the board.

For example, a couple of years ago, owning a share of stock from MoviePass's parent company, Helios and Matheson Analytics, might have provided you with more upside if the company did well, but it also exposed you to losing much more of your original investment if the company's business performed poorly. Helios and Matheson Analytics entered 2017 with a stock price of $820 a share (accounting for stock splits), and reached a stock price high of $5,100 on October 13, 2017, a 522% increase! However, by the summer of 2018, the company's stock price had plummeted to mere pennies, losing nearly 100% of its value. What a wild ride!

On the other hand, let's say you have a portfolio with a little bit invested in a number of different companies. Some companies will do well, and others will not do so well. The strong-performing companies will hopefully outweigh the weak-performing companies to give your portfolio an overall positive investment return. We can see this dynamic play out by looking at the performance of the 100% stock portfolio in Table 12.4. While this portfolio did have a wide variation of returns from year to year (−43% to 54%), that range was relatively small compared to what we saw with Helios and Matheson Analytics.

It's Nearly Impossible to Pick the Winners Consistently

Everyone has that uncle or friend who bought a stock or two at the right time (let's say Microsoft in the '90s, or Facebook in 2012), realized a great return, and can't stop telling you about their experience. After hearing their stories, you might think, "If my idiot brother was able to pick winners, I'm sure I could. I used to beat him at everything, so I surely could beat him at this, too."

But there's a catch: most people only talk about their winners when it comes to investing. Dig deeper, and you'll probably find that they have left a lot of questions unanswered. Sure, they invested in Google in 2004, but how much money did they invest and when did they sell? How'd they do with the rest of their portfolio? They've undoubtedly chosen some losers as well, but those aren't as fun to talk about, so they've conveniently left those details out.

If you were to do a quick online search for a list of the highest-yielding investment categories or asset classes by year, what you'd notice is that no investment category consistently yields the highest returns. Even the ranking of investment categories changes from year to year, with some categories ranking high one year and low the next year. Just think – if it's really hard to predict which asset class will yield the most in any given year, how hard would it be to identify the individual winners *within* an asset class? The answer is: nearly impossible.

In fact, very few people have been able to pick the winners and outperform the market consistently. Peter Lynch, who managed Fidelity's Magellan mutual fund for nearly 15 years, is a rare example of someone who did just that. During his tenure at Fidelity, his fund averaged returns of more than 29% a year – regularly surpassing the S&P 500 return by more than double.[5] And of course there is Warren Buffett, who grew the holding company Berkshire Hathaway an average of more than 20% a year from 1965 to 2018,[6] surpassing the S&P 500 average annual growth of less than 10%.

But most other investors, including those touted as "experts" in the media, have not been so lucky.

One example is American economist Nouriel Roubini, who, in 2005, correctly predicted that the US housing market would collapse and cause a recession within the next few years, earning him the nickname "Dr. Doom." Unfortunately, Roubini has been wrong a number of times since his correct Great Recession call. Perhaps most notably, he predicted another large stock market correction for 2012 or 2013 that never happened.[7] Rather, the S&P 500 returned 16% in 2012, and more than 32% in 2013.

Businesswoman Meredith Whitney is another investing "expert" who hasn't always read the tea leaves accurately. In 2007, she gained fame after correctly predicting that Citigroup would need to cut its dividend. In December 2010, she appeared on *60 Minutes* and famously predicted that there would be 50 to 100 sizable defaults in the municipal market in 2011, amounting to hundreds of billions of dollars of defaults[8] – a bold call. Unfortunately for Whitney, her prediction was way off base. In fact, the municipal bond market had a great year in 2011, returning investors more than 12%.

The lesson? While people may be right about the stock market some of the time – whether by skill, luck, or a combination of both – they are rarely right *all of the time*. Predicting the stock market requires you to know not only what to buy, but when to buy it, and the right time to sell the investment – a tall order. So the next time your uncle, a friend, or the expert on TV gives you advice on a must-buy stock, ask yourself: if this person can predict what stocks will substantially increase in value and when, why are they working at whatever they're doing, rather than using their investment gains to relax on their own island?

How to Build Diversified Portfolios Efficiently Through Mutual Funds and ETFs

At this point, you might be thinking: if investing is such a crapshoot, I probably shouldn't even bother. I'd rather just put my hard-earned money in the bank and call it a day. Plus I *really* don't want to spend my free time studying up on this stuff when I could be on a pizza crawl (or doing anything else, for that matter).

But before you skip ahead to the next chapter, there's another thing you should know: two investment vehicles, mutual funds and exchange-traded funds (ETFs), can allow you to create a well-diversified investment portfolio by buying just one or more funds – giving the average investor a simple way to invest efficiently and reach their goals. Yup, you heard me right.

Mutual funds and ETFs pool money together from many different investors to purchase stocks, bonds, or other assets. Both types of funds offer investors:

- The opportunity to create a diversified investment portfolio
- Low-cost options
- The ability to invest across geographies, sectors, company types and sizes, among other options
- Access to both passively and actively managed investments (we'll come back to this point later)

Yet despite their many similarities, mutual funds and ETFs differ in several important ways. Table 12.6 outlines the key distinctions between these two investment vehicles.

How to Decide Between Mutual Funds and ETFs

If you're liking the sound of mutual funds and ETFs, how do you decide between the two? The following cheat sheet might be helpful as you ponder your options.

You may want to consider mutual funds if you:
- Have sufficient cash to meet mutual fund minimums
- Don't need to buy and sell investments throughout the day
- Prefer to automate ongoing or future purchases

You may want to consider ETFs if you:
- Don't have enough money to meet the investment minimums for mutual funds

Table 12.6 Differences Between Mutual Funds and ETFs.

	Mutual Funds	ETFs
Minimum Investment	Minimum investment varies; some funds have $0 minimums, while others may require an initial investment of $1,000 or more	Require a minimum investment equal to the price of one share, which could be less than $100
Buying and Selling	Can be bought and sold once a day at the close of each trading day	Can be bought and sold throughout the trading day, much like a stock
Transaction Fees	May be subject to fixed transaction fees. Most low-cost index mutual funds may not trade free unless you hold your account directly with the fund issuer. For example, buying and selling a Vanguard mutual fund with a Vanguard account may cost $0, while if bought and sold with a non-Vanguard account, it may cost as much as $50.	Are subject to bid-ask spread fees and may be subject to brokerage commissions. ETFs may be subject to a brokerage commission unless you hold your account directly with the ETF issuer. For example, buying and selling a Vanguard ETF with a Vanguard account may cost $0, while if bought and sold with a non-Vanguard account, it may cost as much as $10.

- Value being able to buy and sell investments throughout the day
- Don't mind having to manually execute ongoing or future purchases

Regardless of which you choose, consider picking a brokerage provider that offers low-cost, proprietary mutual funds and ETFs, such as Vanguard, Fidelity, or Schwab, so you can avoid paying brokerage commissions when you buy and sell your holdings. For example, if you choose to have an account with Fidelity, you will typically pay zero transaction fees for buying and selling most Fidelity mutual funds and ETFs, but could pay up to $50 to buy and sell non-Fidelity mutual funds and ETFs.

Allan Roth, financial planner at Wealth Logic and author of *How a Second Grader Beats Wall Street*, says it's also important to consider a provider's track record and trustworthiness, particularly with a taxable brokerage account. "My first index fund was the S&P 500 index fund from one of the industry giants in the '80s and '90s that later raised its fees (now clocking in at 0.50% compared to 0.05% or less for equivalent funds) leaving me with the miserable choice of staying put and continuing to pay higher fees or selling and being taxed on my profits by the IRS." That's why Roth recommends Vanguard mutual funds and ETFs for his clients.

Passive versus Active Investing

As I touched on before, both mutual funds and ETFs offer you the opportunity to employ either a passive or an active investment strategy. But what does that mean exactly?

Passive management involves simply trying to track and closely match the investments of a particular market index, while actively managed funds are trying to earn a higher return than the market indexes and benchmarks. For example, a mutual fund or ETF that sought to track the S&P 500 Index would be considered a passively managed fund (and is often referred to as an index fund). Portfolio managers of an S&P 500 index fund would make sure the index fund tracked the S&P Index by selling the stock of companies leaving the index, buying the stock of companies entering the index, and ensuring the proportions of stock in the index fund aligned with the proportions in the S&P 500 Index.

In contrast, actively managed funds are not simply trying to replicate a market index or capture the market return. Rather, they are aiming to beat the market return by performing extensive research and analysis, conferring with potential companies, developing theories on what investments they think will outperform the market, and ultimately executing on those hypotheses.

Deciding whether you're going to employ a passive or an active investment strategy is an important question you'll have to ask yourself, and a decision that could have a big impact on your bottom line. So where does that leave the typical investor (i.e., you're neither a stock market junkie nor are you sitting on piles of excess cash)?

More often than not, I think passive investing through mutual funds or ETFs is the smart approach for the bulk of your investment portfolio. Although an actively managed strategy is clearly more hands-on, that extra effort doesn't always translate into better long-term returns. In fact, a lot of the research suggests the exact *opposite*. S&P Dow Jones Indices has been diligently tracking active versus passive fund performance for 16 years and in its 2018 year-end SPIVA Scorecard found that the S&P 500 Index outperformed nearly 65% of actively managed large-cap funds over a one-year period. Looking at longer time periods only tilted the pendulum more in favor of passive investing, with the S&P 500 Index outperforming nearly 92% of actively managed large-cap funds over a 15-year period.[9]

With so few actively managed funds able to consistently outperform their respective market benchmarks, it can be extremely difficult to identify, in advance, which active funds will deliver higher returns. And with the extra staff and legwork needed, actively managed funds generally charge much higher fees than passively managed funds, and are less tax-efficient. With that said, there may be certain instances when actively managed funds may be appropriate, such as if a low-cost index fund does not exist for a particular asset class, or if an active fund charges a lower fee than the equivalent index fund.

As you begin to think about what investment strategy may be the right fit for you, know that the choice between passive and active investing doesn't need to be an either/or decision. Even if you choose to use a passive investment strategy for the majority of your portfolio, you could still add an actively managed fund or even a couple of individual stocks into the mix. In fact, I typically allow my clients to have up to 5% of their investment portfolio in "play money" to do just that – a strategy that keeps people on track to reach their financial goals with the majority of their portfolio, while giving them some flexibility to be "active" and maybe get lucky.

Where You Can Put Each Investment (Asset Location)

Once you've gotten a handle of your investment options, the next step is to figure out *where* to put each investment – and I don't mean deciding whether to park your money at Fidelity or eTrade. Rather, you will need to understand the different account types available to you and how they work to determine which accounts may be appropriate for you.

There are three main types of investment buckets where you can hold investments:

- **Tax-Deferred (or Pretax)**: Contributions are made on a pretax basis (read: investing money that hasn't been taxed) and lower your taxable income in the current year by your contribution amount. When withdrawn, funds are taxed as income. Examples of pretax accounts include a 401(k), 403(b), and traditional IRA.
- **Tax-Free (or Roth)**: Contributions are made on an after-tax basis (read: investing money that has been taxed) and don't lower your current year taxable income. Withdrawals taken at retirement are generally not taxable. Examples of tax-free accounts include a Roth 401(k) and Roth IRA.
- **Taxable**: Contributions are made with money that has already been taxed (similar to a Roth IRA or Roth 401(k)). Income from investments, such as interest and dividends, are taxable in the year received (even if reinvested) and capital gains (appreciation in the price of the investment) are taxable in the year the investment is sold.

You may be most familiar with the pretax bucket, especially if you are working for a company and participating in your employer's retirement plan. The pretax contribution type is the default option for many retirement plans,[10] and for those plans with automatic enrollment, the pretax contribution type is typically selected.[11] With that said, the tax-free bucket is becoming more readily available in company plans. Fidelity's "Building Financial Futures" quarterly report found that nearly 70% of plans that it administers were offering employees the option of contributing to their retirement plans on a Roth basis as of the first quarter of 2019 – a substantial increase from the first quarter of 2014, when just 46% of Fidelity retirement plans offered the Roth option.[12] However, the utilization of Roth contributions is still fairly small, with just 11% of participants using this contribution type when given the option.[13]

Pretax or Roth?

One question you're trying to answer when deciding whether to contribute to your retirement account on a pretax or Roth basis is whether you'd be better off paying taxes today (Roth contributions) or waiting until you withdraw money in retirement (pretax contributions).

A key input is your marginal tax bracket, which determines the amount of current year tax savings you'll reap for pretax contributions or how much in taxes you'll owe for Roth contributions. As you progress to higher tax brackets, you'll realize greater current year tax savings for pretax contributions and increased taxes owed for Roth contributions.

Consider a scenario where you have $10,000 to contribute to your 401(k). If you were in the 10% marginal tax bracket, making a pretax contribution would mean saving $1,000 in taxes in the current year ($10,000 × 10%), while a Roth contribution would mean having to pay that $1,000 in taxes today. If you were in the 37% marginal tax bracket, the numbers get much larger – a pretax contribution would equate to saving $3,700 in current year taxes ($10,000 × 37%), while a Roth contribution would mean having to pay that $3,700 tax bill today.

With perfect information about your career trajectory, future income, and future tax rates, you could simply model out the most efficient decision in a spreadsheet. Unfortunately, we don't have information that is even close to perfect. Most of us have no idea what the trajectory of our careers will be, how long we'll be working, and how much we'll be making – let alone the future direction of tax rates (and if you do know, call me!).

That unpredictability is why having tax diversification, or money spread across investment buckets (i.e., pretax, tax-free, and taxable), is important as well. In the past, most people just threw as much money as they could into the pretax bucket. While withdrawals from pretax accounts are taxed at your marginal tax rate, many assumed they would be in a lower tax bracket in retirement. However, that may not be the case at all.

The US government requires people to withdraw money from their pretax retirement accounts beginning in their early 70s, whether they need to or not, through required minimum distributions. For example, a 74-year-old with a 401(k) balance of $1.5 million would be required to withdraw $63,000 from their pretax account, according to a required minimum distribution calculator from Investor.gov. Add in Social Security and other fixed taxable income, and you can see how you may be on your way to a much higher tax bracket than you anticipated. The withdrawals from pretax accounts affect not only your tax bracket but also could impact your Medicare Part B and D premium amounts, and the portion of your Social Security benefits that are subject to tax. What a major bummer!

Spreading money across investment buckets can help you combat some of these dynamics by giving "future you" flexibility to pull money from pretax, tax-free, or taxable accounts, allowing you to better control your tax bracket in retirement (read: save money).

When deciding whether to contribute to your retirement accounts on a pretax or Roth basis from year to year, you can use the following guidelines as a starting point. However, if your money is overly concentrated in one investment bucket, you may consider straying from the guidelines to diversify your investment buckets.

When to consider a Roth contribution (i.e., pay taxes today):
- You are a recent graduate and expect your salary to increase as you progress in your career.
- You only worked for a portion of the year.
- You're in a relatively low tax bracket (i.e., 10% or 12% for 2019).

When to consider a pretax contribution (i.e., pay taxes later):
- You are in one of the highest tax brackets (i.e., 32%, 35%, or 37% for 2019).
- You already contribute the maximum amount to your 401(k) and have the option and available cashflow to contribute to Roth accounts using the mega-backdoor Roth IRA and/or backdoor Roth IRA strategies.

What You Pay to Invest (Fees and Expenses)

What you pay to invest matters tremendously. In 2015, the wealth management company Personal Capital conducted a study on the total fees people paid to large investment managers (see Table 12.7).[14] The study incorporated fees that you pay to your financial advisor (i.e., assets under management fees), as well as the underlying fees on the actual investments (e.g., expense ratios, in the case of mutual funds and ETFs). Personal Capital found that some of the largest brokerage houses and household names charged as much as 2% in total fees per year!

Your Return = Fund Return – Costs

Now you might be thinking, "Paying 2% in fees doesn't sound that bad. Heck, it seems like a small price to pay to ensure the other

Table 12.7   Average All-In Investment Fees by Investment Manager type.

Provider	All-in-Fee (as % of Investment Balance Managed)	Annual Fee (Assuming a $500,000 Balance)
Low-Cost Providers	0.08% to 0.15%	$400 to $750
Robo-Advisors	0.35% to 0.55%	$1,750 to $2,750
Large Brokerage Houses	1.00% to 2.00%	$5,000 to $10,000

Source: Adapted from a study performed by Personal Capital. Note that Low-Cost Providers and Robo-Advisors were not part of the original analysis.

98% of my money is well-managed." But consider this: if you pay 2% in fees, you would need your investment portfolio to return *at least* 2% a year just to break even. If the overall market returned 7% in a year, your portfolio would need to earn 9% just to match the market return.

Setting aside your financial advisor's performance, investment fees can add up – and quickly. For example, on a $500,000 investment portfolio, a 2% fee would equate to $10,000 a year that you'd pay year after year – and that amount would increase as your portfolio grew in value! Table 12.7 also includes low-cost providers and robo-advisors that charge lower fees. If you were to put your $500,000 portfolio into one of these options instead, your annual fees would be $400 to $2,750 – a pretty big savings compared to $10,000!

With many products and services, the old adage "You get what you pay for" may hold true. However, with investing, Jack Bogle said, "You get what you don't pay for."[15] This is important to keep in mind on your investment journey because many factors that can impact your investment returns are beyond your control, like market performance, but what you pay to invest is well within your control. While fees can vary widely depending on who is managing your money, and what they have you invested in, if you are aiming to use predominantly passively managed index funds, those funds should have expense ratios of 0.25% or less.

Can I Start Investing My Money Yet?

The bottom line is, investing starts with you – having a good understanding of what goals you want to achieve, when you want to achieve those goals, and how much risk you can stomach along the way matters more than anything going on in the market.

What you invest in will be heavily influenced by what you're investing for. Where to put each of your investments will depend on what account types you have available. Regardless of what you're investing for, it's important to be mindful of how much you're paying to invest. Minimizing fees is one factor that is well within your control and can materially impact your net investment return.

In the next chapter, we'll apply the concepts we've walked through to explore how you can balance efficiency and simplicity to create an investment portfolio that is right for you.

Chapter 13
How to Construct Your Portfolio

Can you relate to this situation? It's Wednesday afternoon, you've lost steam at work, and your lunch break just ended. What a drag. Naturally, you put aside that ASAP assignment you were supposed to finish yesterday to spend a few minutes focusing on more appetizing thoughts – like what you should do for dinner.

Your first option is to go all in, Bobby Flay style. This would entail heading to the grocery store after work, purchasing the individual ingredients you need to make a nice meal, sous chefing, cooking, and cleaning up afterward. That may be the cheapest and tastiest option, but it also takes up most of your evening.

Alternatively, you could pay a little more for precut vegetables to avoid having to spend 15 minutes chopping onions and wiping away your tears – and still get most of the benefits of a home-cooked meal.

Or finally, because it's a weekday, you could just pick up a meal from the prepared foods section – requiring you to simply reheat and eat, and freeing up time for you to watch a movie. While this option may be the priciest and the least tasty, it requires minimal preparation and cleanup.

Believe it or not, the thought process you go through to decide how to prepare a meal parallels deciding how to build your investment portfolio. In both cases, multiple options are available that will get you to the same destination (i.e., nourished or properly invested). However, the cost and time commitment required for each option will vary.

When deciding between your options for cooking and investing, you're trying to balance efficiency and simplicity. The underlying ingredients you choose to use in your meal or investment portfolio can simplify or complicate your meal preparation or investment plan. Ingredients that simplify either will likely cost a little more.

In both situations, there is no one-size-fits-all option that will be right for everyone. People with a greater interest in cooking or investments may gravitate toward the more hands-on, time-intensive options. Those who are less interested may choose to pay more for simpler options requiring little cleanup or ongoing management.

In this chapter, you'll learn how to balance efficiency and simplicity when investing, and how to construct an investment portfolio that aligns with your goals and the amount of time you want to spend managing your investments.

Step 1: Complete Prerequisites

Which investments you use in your portfolio will depend on **what** goals you want to achieve and **when** you want to achieve them. If you haven't fully formed your goals, please refer back to Chapter 11 and go through the exercises to define, quantify, and prioritize your goals.

In Chapter 11, two mandatory goals that I mention include saving for an emergency fund and paying off high-cost debt, such as credit card debt and personal loans. If you haven't funded an emergency fund and fully paid off high-cost debt, focus on achieving those goals before dipping your toe into investing. Reaching both goals will help you build a solid financial foundation and ensure you can stick to your investment plan.

Step 2: Review Your Goals

Once you've completed the prerequisites for investing, the next step toward building your investment portfolio is to review your goals and the applicable timelines for each. Table 13.1 provides general guidance on how to invest your money, based on your time horizon for a particular goal.

When saving for goals less than five years away, most of the allocated money should remain in cash. While this strategy will limit your potential gains, it will also limit your potential losses, giving you a better chance of having the money you'll need to achieve these short-term goals. For goals that are five or more years away, the exercise requires a little more thought. As your time horizon increases, you may feel more comfortable increasing your stock exposure. In order to determine the right asset allocation for you, you'll need to evaluate and balance the trade-offs between how much risk you want or need to take, compared to the expected return (see Table 13.2).

In particular, your personal risk tolerance could influence your ability and comfort sticking with your plan and investment portfolio, especially in the face of large downward swings in prices. While stocks may return, on average, positive annual returns for longer holding periods, the journey to capturing those long-term positive returns may feel more like riding a rollercoaster than floating along a lazy river – with a lot of bumps along the way, and potentially huge

Table 13.1 Directional Investment Guidelines Based on Goal Time Frames.

Time Frame for Goal	Example Goals	Investment Guideline
Less than five years	Vacation, car, home, continuing education	Mostly cash (e.g., high-yield savings account, certificate of deposit, or equivalent holding)
Five to 15 years	College savings	A mix of bonds and stocks
15-plus years	Retirement/financial independence	Mostly stocks

Table 13.2 Considerations for Whether to Invest in More Stocks.

Consideration	Guideline
Time frame	Shorter-term goals should be tilted more toward bonds; as your time frame increases, you can introduce more stock exposure.
Flexibility of time frame	If your time frame is set, you may not want to take as much risk; if your time frame is flexible and can be delayed, you may be able to take on more risk.
Risk tolerance	If you get spooked easily because of large downward swings in the market, you may want to take on less risk.
Need for returns	Based on your existing savings and how much you can save on an ongoing basis, do you need a high return to reach your goal? If not, you may want to consider taking on less stock exposure.

downward swings in your portfolio value. If severe market downturns could cause you to make knee-jerk reactions, such as moving all of your money to cash, you may be more comfortable with a lower percentage of stocks in your portfolio – even if your goal is 20-plus years away.

While there isn't a perfect way to measure risk tolerance, some firms use questionnaires focused on your past or potential actions in turbulent markets to gauge your comfort level with risk. You can find and use a free online risk tolerance questionnaire by doing a quick online search. These risk tolerance questionnaires may be a good starting point to figure out your approximate risk tolerance, and give you more clarity about what the right mix of stocks and bonds may be for you and your goals.

But before you spend hours upon hours trying to figure out the perfect apportionment of your assets, remember that solving for your asset allocation isn't like solving a math problem in school. There is no one "correct" allocation for a particular goal because everyone has different preferences, risk tolerances, and financial situations. Furthermore, a 5% to 10% difference in your stock or bond allocations won't make a significant financial difference to you in the long run. The difference in the Vanguard analysis of average annual returns for various mixes of stocks and bonds was about 0.3% to 0.5% for a 10% change in stock exposure – not a big deal in the grand scheme of things.

How to Maintain Your Asset Allocation and Rebalance Your Portfolio

The asset allocation (i.e., your mix of stocks, bonds, and other investments) that you start out with at the beginning of the year will likely not be the same allocation you have at the end of the year because of changes in the market. In fact, the mix of stocks and bonds in your portfolio may shift the day after you execute on your strategy as the underlying investments in your portfolio will probably perform differently; stocks may increase in value and bonds may drop in value, or vice versa. Over time, these fluctuations may shift the proportion of stocks and bonds in your portfolio so that they no longer align with your target, causing your portfolio to become either more or less risky than you'd like. This is why periodic rebalancing is important.

You can take either a time-based or value-based approach to rebalancing your portfolio. Time-based rebalancing means holding yourself to a set schedule of when to rebalance your portfolio, like semi-annually or annually.

Value-based rebalancing means that instead of rebalancing on a set schedule, you would rebalance your portfolio when your mix of stocks and bonds reached a certain percentage above or below your target asset allocation. For example, let's say you decided to rebalance your portfolio whenever your stock allocation had deviated more than 10% above or below your target. If your target allocation to stocks was 80%, you would rebalance your portfolio

(continued)

(*continued*)

whenever your allocation moved to 90% stocks or more, or 70% stocks or less.

While there is no "right" or "best" way to rebalance your portfolio, most readers managing their own portfolios may lean toward the time-based rebalancing approach because it is more hands-off and automatic. In this approach, you'll still compare your actual allocation to your target allocation on rebalancing dates. If the differences are minor, you may decide not to rebalance at all. The value-based strategy, on the other hand, requires you to monitor your portfolio more closely.

In order to rebalance, you would typically sell the holding that you have too much of and buy more of the holding that you don't have enough of. Let's revisit the prior example in which your target stock allocation had increased from 80% stocks to 90% stocks. In this case, you would need to sell stocks and buy more bonds so your allocations again matched your targets. Alternatively, if you continued to add money to your investment accounts throughout the year, you could simply buy more of the holding that had decreased in value (i.e., bonds in this case), and less of the excessive holding (i.e., stocks in this example).

Selling holdings to rebalance your portfolio in a pretax or Roth account won't have any immediate tax implications. However, if you are selling holdings that have gained value in a taxable brokerage account, you may incur capital gains taxes on this selling, so the tax implications of rebalancing in your taxable account is something to be mindful of before proceeding.

If rebalancing sounds like a lot of work, using target-date funds, which I'll discuss shortly, may be a good fit because these funds do the rebalancing for you, so you don't have to think about how, when, or how often you should rebalance your portfolio.

Step 3: Evaluate Your Options

Once you've determined your overarching mix of stocks and bonds (i.e., your asset allocation), you can take action and implement that target asset allocation in a number of ways, including through a one-fund portfolio, a three-fund portfolio, an asset-located portfolio, or some variation of these portfolios.

Structurally, these options differ based on 1) the number of funds you'll use and 2) whether you'll maintain the same funds in the same proportion across accounts. Those factors will influence the complexity of your portfolio and ongoing management required, as well as how efficient your portfolio is from a cost and tax perspective. Let's take a closer look at each of these options.

Option 1: One-Fund Portfolio (Target-Date Fund)

Translation: All accounts would use the same one fund in the same proportion.

A one-fund portfolio allows you to achieve your target stock and bond mix simply by purchasing one fund, instead of having to buy three or more funds to achieve the same allocation. These funds are sometimes referred to as target-date or lifecycle funds, with most funds having names that may include "Target Retirement Fund [Year]" or "Target [Year]" (see Table 13.3). Generally, target-date funds with years that are further away from the current year will have a greater proportion of stocks than those funds with years that are closer to the current year. For example, the Vanguard Target Retirement 2050 fund has 90% stocks,[1] compared with its 2030 Target Retirement fund, which is made up of 75% stocks.[2]

Not only do target-date funds simplify the upfront selection process, but they also take care of the ongoing portfolio management. Specifically, they rebalance the portfolio to the target asset allocation while also decreasing the exposure to stocks in the fund as you approach the target retirement date – a task you would be otherwise responsible for handling or outsourcing.

Table 13.3   Target-Date Fund Naming Convention and Fees.

Fund family	Target-Date Fund Naming Convention (Passively Managed Funds)	Expense Ratio Range
Fidelity	Fidelity Freedom Index [Year] Fund	0.08% to 0.14%
Schwab	Schwab Target [Year] Index Fund	0.08%
Vanguard	Target Retirement [Year]	0.12% to 0.15%

Target-date funds may be a good fit for you if:
- You value simplicity above all else.
- You want to do minimal maintenance and ongoing management of your portfolio.
- You only have one investment account at the moment, such as a company 401(k).
- You're not currently investing in a taxable brokerage account.
- You may not have enough money to meet investment minimums of multiple mutual funds.

Target-date funds may NOT be a good fit for you if:
- You have money spread across multiple account types, especially if one of those accounts includes a taxable brokerage account.
- You value paying the lowest fees possible.

A Warning About Target-Date Fund Fees
While many fund families offer passively managed target-date funds, some fund families offer both passively managed and actively managed target-date funds. The actively managed target-date funds are much more expensive, so be sure to check the expense ratio of a fund before making a purchase.

For example, Fidelity's actively managed 2050 fund is called "Fidelity Freedom 2050 Fund"[3] while its passively managed fund is called "Fidelity Freedom Index 2050 Fund."[4] The only difference in the names is that the passively managed fund includes the word "index" in its name. The difference in fees, though, is huge – the actively managed version has an expense ratio of 0.75% compared to just 0.08% for the passively managed version. For most of the large fund families, like Vanguard, Fidelity, and Schwab, the passively managed target-date funds have expense ratios of 0.20% or less, and several have expense ratios less than 0.10%.

Option 2: Three-Fund Portfolio

Translation: All accounts would use the same three or more funds in the same proportion.

In a three-fund portfolio structure, which was originated by Taylor Larimore and popularized by the Bogleheads, instead of buying just one mutual fund or ETF, you would buy three or more funds to achieve your target allocation. Typically, the three funds would consist of a total US stock market index fund, a total international stock market index fund, and a total US bond market index fund.

To determine the amount of money to allocate to each fund, you would first figure out your overall target allocation of stocks and bonds based on your goals, timeline, and risk tolerance. Then you would need to determine how to segment your stock allocation between US and international index funds. While your exact mix will depend on your individual preferences, many leading experts recommend having 20% to 50% of your stock allocation in international stock index funds. You may also refer to the investment breakdown used by target-date funds for additional guidance on how to determine your mix of US and international stock funds.

While implementing the three-fund portfolio structure is pretty straightforward if you only have one account, if you had multiple investment accounts, such as a 401(k) and a taxable brokerage account, you could use the same mix of stocks and bonds in each. For example, in the scenario that you had both a 401(k) and a taxable brokerage account with a target allocation of 90% stocks and 10% bonds, you would buy three funds in each account such that your allocation would be 90% stocks and 10% bonds in your 401(k), and 90% stocks and 10% bonds in your taxable brokerage account.

On an ongoing basis, you would be on the hook for periodically rebalancing your portfolio to ensure your mix of stocks and bonds in each account was close or equal to your original targets. As you approached your goal target, you would also be responsible for gradually decreasing the proportion of stocks in your portfolio.

The upsides of this added complexity are increased flexibility and lower expenses compared with a low-cost target-date fund. For example, the Vanguard Target Retirement 2050 fund has an expense ratio of 0.15%.[1] This option consists of four underlying Vanguard funds:

- Vanguard Total Stock Market Index Fund Investor Shares
- Vanguard Total International Stock Index Fund Investor Shares
- Vanguard Total Bond Market II Index Fund
- Vanguard Total International Bond Index Fund

If you bought these (or similar) funds individually and in the same proportion as the Target Retirement 2050 fund, you would only pay 0.07% in ongoing expenses, instead of 0.15%. However, this strategy requires overcoming certain hurdles. In particular, you would need to have sufficient money to meet the minimum investment for each fund (outside of your retirement plan), typically starting at $1,000 or higher.

Table 13.4 provides examples of funds people often use to build a three-fund portfolio with different fund families:

Table 13.4   Example Funds Often Used to Construct a Three-Fund Portfolio.

Fund Family	US Stock Fund	International Stock Fund	US Bond Market Fund
Fidelity	Fidelity Total Market Index Fund (FSKAX)	Fidelity Total International Index Fund (FTIHX)	Fidelity US Bond Index Fund (FXNAX)
Schwab	Schwab Total Stock Market Index Fund (SWTSX)	Schwab International Index Fund (SWISX)	Schwab US Aggregate Bond Index Fund (SWAGX)
Vanguard	Vanguard Total Stock Market Index Admiral Shares (VTSAX)	Vanguard Total International Stock Index Admiral Shares (VTIAX)	Vanguard Total Bond Market Index Admiral Shares (VBTLX)

A three-fund portfolio structure may be a good fit for you if:

- You have money spread across several different account types, including a taxable brokerage account.
- You want to pay the lowest fees possible.
- You can meet the investment minimum for multiple mutual funds (outside of your retirement plan) or choose to use ETFs.

A three-fund portfolio structure may NOT be a good fit for you if:

- You value simplicity above all else.
- You only have one account type, and it's a pretax or Roth account, not a taxable brokerage account.
- You want to use mutual funds, but are unable to meet the investment minimums for several mutual funds.

Option 3: Asset-Located Portfolio

Translation: Use three or more funds across accounts (like the three-fund portfolio), but each account may have different funds in different proportions.

An asset-located portfolio builds on the fundamentals of the three-fund portfolio structure. Like the three-fund portfolio, an asset-located portfolio would require you to buy three or more funds to reach your target allocation, and you would be responsible for the ongoing rebalancing and risk management of your portfolio. However, unlike a three-fund portfolio structure, where you maintained the same mix of stocks and bonds across account types (e.g., 90% stocks and 10% bonds in your 401(k), and 90% stocks and 10% bonds in your taxable brokerage account), you would unlikely use the same allocation in each account type with an asset-located portfolio (see Table 13.5). Instead, you would focus on placing the most tax-efficient investments in your taxable brokerage account, and the least tax-efficient investments in either your pretax or Roth accounts.

Tax-efficient investments are those that would generally provide you with investment income subject to the more advantageous long-term capital gains rates in a taxable account (read: a lower tax rate). Tax-inefficient investments would be those that kick off investment income subject to the higher short-term capital gains rates (a.k.a. your marginal tax rate – read: much higher tax rates).

- **Tax-Efficient Investments**: Total stock market index funds, tax-managed stock funds, small-cap or mid-cap index funds
- **Tax-Inefficient Investments**: Taxable bonds, REIT funds, actively managed funds

If you were in the 32% tax bracket and received $1,000 in income from your taxable investments, you'd net $680 if the income was interest from a taxable bond and would clear $850 if the income was qualified dividends from a total stock market fund – a $170 difference.

Table 13.5   Executing a 90% Stock/10% Bond Allocation ($200k Portfolio).

	Three-Fund Portfolio	Asset-Located Portfolio
Account: 401(k) **Amount**: $100,000	$90k Stocks (90%) $10k Bonds (10%)	$80k Stocks (80%) $20k Bonds (20%)
Account: Taxable Brokerage **Amount**: $100,000	$90k Stocks (90%) $10k Bonds (10%)	$100k Stocks (100%)
Total Portfolio **Amount: $200,000**	$180k Stocks (90%) $20k Bonds (10%)	$180k Stocks (90%) $20k Bonds (20%)

While being deliberate about which investments you put in what account is certainly the most cost and tax-efficient, it also requires the most amount of work. Because each account may not have the same mix of stocks and bonds by design, it will be difficult to see if your overall asset allocation is off simply by looking at your account. For this strategy, you'll likely need to use a spreadsheet to outline your target allocation across accounts. The other difficulty with this strategy is your account types (e.g., pretax, Roth, and taxable) will likely accumulate money at different rates, making it hard to simply set it and forget it.

An asset-located portfolio may be a good fit for you if:
- You want to pay the lowest fees possible.
- You want your portfolio to be the most tax-efficient.
- You can meet the investment minimum for multiple mutual funds or choose to use ETFs.
- You don't mind having to do ongoing management of your portfolio, and may even enjoy it.
- You have multiple account types, including a taxable brokerage account.
- You're in one of the higher tax brackets (i.e., 32%, 35%, or 37%).

An asset-located portfolio may NOT be a good fit for you if:
- You value simplicity.
- You only have a pretax or Roth account, and no taxable brokerage account.
- You're in a lower tax bracket (i.e., 10%, 12%, or 22%).
- You want to use mutual funds, but are unable to meet the investment minimums for several mutual funds.

What About Robo-Advisors?

Since arriving on the investing scene after the 2008 recession, robo-advisors – automated investment platforms that help investors build and manage investment portfolios – have marketed themselves and attracted new investors to

(continued)

(continued)

good effect. They often position themselves as an alternative to a financial advisor with benefits such as easy account set-up, ongoing rebalancing, tax-loss harvesting, and in some cases, tax-efficient placement of assets. In exchange, robo-advisors typically charge an ongoing management fee of 0.20% to 0.40%, in addition to the fees for the underlying investments – much lower than the fees of a traditional financial advisor, which generally range from 1.00% to 1.50%.

Despite these advantages, the question of whether to use a robo-advisor isn't necessarily so clear-cut. Here are some considerations when deciding whether a robo-advisor should manage your money.

- **Your Needs**: The first factor to consider is your needs—which requires having a clear handle on your current situation. As a first step, figure out how much money you have available to invest, as well as the account types your money is sitting in (e.g., pretax, Roth, taxable). This information will help you determine what type of service would benefit you the most.

  In particular, ask yourself if you're looking to: a) automate and optimize your investments (in which case, a robo-advisor may be a good fit), b) work with someone who can help you with all aspects of your financial situation (which a financial advisor would do), or c) simply manage your investments yourself?

- **Applicable Benefits**: Some robo-advisor benefits may apply to all customers, including automated rebalancing and the use of low-cost investments. However, two benefits often highlighted – tax-loss harvesting and tax-efficient placement of assets – may not apply to your situation if you are only investing money in a traditional or Roth IRA.

Both strategies benefit those investing monies in a taxable brokerage account. Tax-loss harvesting allows you to potentially decrease your tax liability in the current year by selling investments in your taxable account that have temporarily gone down in value at a loss to offset your other investment gains or income that would otherwise be subject to tax. Tax-efficient placement of investments focuses on putting the most tax-efficient assets in your taxable brokerage account—a strategy that is not applicable if you only have money in a traditional or Roth IRA.

- **Costs**: Robo-advisors are less expensive than traditional financial advisors, but they are still more costly than the do-it-yourself portfolios I highlighted in this chapter—including three-fund and asset-located portfolios that would require you to do ongoing rebalancing and risk management of your portfolio, as well as a one-fund portfolio (i.e., a target-date fund) that would take care of those responsibilities for you.
- **Flexibility and Future Options**: The amount of flexibility you want now or in the future matters as well. If you start investing with a robo-advisor with just a traditional or Roth IRA, it's relatively painless, financially, to move this money to a do-it-yourself option or financial advisor down the road because there won't be immediate tax consequences for selling those investments. However, if you use a robo-advisor for your taxable brokerage account, you may incur taxes if your investments increase in value and you decide to change your holdings or strategy.

The bottom line is, robo-advisors offer several potential advantages when it comes to money management, but they're not for everyone. The decision of whether to use a

(continued)

(*continued*)

robo-advisor largely depends on your current situation, the level of help you're seeking, the amount of flexibility you want, and whether the applicable benefits of a robo-advisor outweigh the additional costs.

If you're just starting out and only have a traditional or Roth IRA, that could be a good time to test the waters with a robo-advisor. While you won't realize the benefits of tax-loss harvesting and tax-efficient placement of assets, you'll have the option to move your money to a do-it-yourself option or financial advisor later with little to no tax consequences. A target-date fund could be an excellent alternative for that situation as well, particularly for people who want to get started investing with minimum costs and maintenance.

How to Choose an Investment Strategy That Works for You: Balancing Efficiency and Simplicity

Table 13.6 summarizes the benefits and considerations of the three strategies you could use as the foundation for your investment portfolio. As you're considering which option to use, keep the following questions in mind, which may help you decide the strategy to either start with, or move to.

- Where is your money? Is it in one account type, like a 401(k), or spread across multiple account types, such as a 401(k), Roth IRA, and taxable brokerage account?
- How much flexibility do you want now or in the future to potentially make your portfolio more cost and tax-efficient?
- How important is it to you to keep costs and taxes low?
- How much ongoing work are you willing to do (i.e., rebalancing and other management)?

When determining which strategy to use, you'll want to balance two competing priorities: efficiency and simplicity.

As your portfolio becomes more efficient from a cost and tax perspective, it will also become more complex and take more time to manage on an ongoing basis. The simplest portfolio includes having just one fund – which is easy to track, and doesn't require much ongoing management or intervention. The trade-off for that simplicity is you will pay a slightly higher fee, you may lose some flexibility, and you could have a less tax-efficient portfolio.

Some people, like my friend Alberto, are super interested in personal finance and want to be very hands-on with their investment portfolio, so they choose a more complex portfolio implementation that requires a fair amount of upkeep. Others may think of investing as just another item on their to-do list that they need to tackle, and don't want it to consume their lives. If you fall into the latter bucket, having a one-fund portfolio may be totally fine. You'll get close to the market return, can rest easy that you're invested properly, and will still pay low fees compared to investors who use a financial advisor or actively managed funds.

Table 13.6   Summary of Base Portfolio Structures.

	Option 1: One-Fund Portfolio (Target-Date Fund)	Option 2: Three-Fund Portfolio	Option 3: Asset-Located Portfolio
Translation	All accounts would use the same one fund in the same proportion.	All accounts would use the same three or more funds in the same proportion.	Use three or more funds across accounts (like the three-fund portfolio), but each account may have different funds in different proportions.
# of Funds	1	3-plus	3-plus
Complexity	Least	Somewhat	Most
Ongoing Rebalancing & Management	Least Work	Some Work	Most Work
Flexibility	Least Flexible	Most Flexible	Most Flexible
Cost	Most Expensive	Least Expensive	Least Expensive
Tax-Efficiency	Least Tax-Efficient	Potentially More Tax-Efficient	Most Tax-Efficient

Your Strategy Can Change

The strategy you decide on today doesn't have to be the strategy you stick with forever. Circumstances change, and what was best for you in your 20s may not be ideal later down the road. That's exactly the message David Oransky, financial planner at Laminar Wealth, tells those who want to manage their own investment portfolios.

"If you're new to investing and have no taxable accounts, a one-fund portfolio could be a good way to get started, and still leaves open the option to change your strategy in the future with minimal consequences," Oransky says. That's because with pretax and Roth accounts, it's relatively easy to pivot strategies and move money within those accounts without incurring taxes today.

Having investments in a taxable brokerage account begins to complicate matters because as you sell holdings in a taxable account that grow in value, you could pay hefty taxes. This is why Rick Ferri, financial advisor and author of *All About Asset Allocation*, among other books, says, "Make sure you're absolutely in love with the equity mutual funds and ETFs you decide to put into your taxable account because like marriage, divorcing yourself from those holdings later can often be a taxing experience."

If you're a novice investor and have a taxable account, Oransky thinks the three-fund portfolio strategy could be a good way to start investing more efficiently, while giving you the flexibility to move to an asset-located portfolio strategy in the future. "If you start with a three-fund portfolio strategy in each of your accounts and down the road decide it's worthwhile to asset-locate across your accounts, you could likely sell the bond fund in your taxable account with little to no capital gains tax," he says.

Bottom line: your investment strategy can and likely will change over time as you add more money and different accounts to your portfolio. Changing strategies and selling investments within your pretax and Roth accounts should be relatively seamless, with no immediate tax implications. Even selling bond holdings within your taxable account should have a minimal tax impact, but be mindful of the equity holdings you buy and sell in your taxable account, as those tax implications may not be as minor.

Chapter 14

Protecting Your Wealth

September 21, 2016, began like any other workday for Sharon Epperson. Before heading to her job as CNBC's Senior Personal Finance Correspondent, Epperson had breakfast with her family, got the kids to school, and slipped in a workout. That's when the day turned into one that Epperson would never forget.

After experiencing severe neck and head pain while working out, she knew something was wrong and called her husband immediately. Once at the hospital, the doctors determined Epperson had a ruptured brain aneurysm – a condition that's fatal in 50% of cases and leaves 66% of survivors with some permanent neurological deficit, according to the Brain Aneurysm Foundation.[1]

"Without warning, I was suddenly disabled, and uncertain of if or when I would ever be able to return to my career," says Epperson.

Fortunately, after a year of rehabilitation, Epperson was able to make a full recovery and return to work. Nevertheless, she says that she benefited immensely from having an estate plan and the right insurance.

"Looking back, I am relieved I had the estate planning tools in place that allowed my family to make critical health care and financial decisions on my behalf, as well as the appropriate insurance coverage that ensured our expenses were covered while I was unable to work," Epperson explains.

This may not be the most fun topic, but equipping yourself with the right tools to protect your human and financial capital is an essential step in any financial plan. Left unprotected, one unfortunate incident could wipe out all of your money – and with it, the hard work you have put into finding the right career and optimizing your finances.

Insurance and estate planning are the two strategies that most people rely on to protect their financial stability. But unlike most other goods and services you'll ever purchase, neither of these tools provides an immediate tangible return. Both enable you and your family to proactively prepare for an unfortunate event that will hopefully never transpire, such as an accident, disability, or even death.

While insurance and estate planning can be complicated to navigate, they can be your best line of defense against unexpected financial detriment, especially if you ask yourself the right questions along the way. In this chapter, we'll break down the main types of insurance and estate planning tools, as well as the key considerations for deciding if and how to use them, so that you can come away with a clear action plan for protecting your wealth.

Insurance

Insurance helps protect our assets from a variety of risks that we all face in our day-to-day lives. Some risks are more likely to happen than others. For example, I'm probably more likely to be hit by a car than be struck by lightning (especially walking through the streets of New York City, where I live). Risks also vary in their negative impact to us. Getting severely injured or dying in a car accident has much more severe consequences for me and my family than tripping on a crack in the sidewalk.

When it comes to insurance planning, ***the rule of thumb is to buy insurance for risks that are unlikely to happen, but would have devastating financial consequences if they did occur.***

The types of insurance you need will depend on what you own and if anyone depends on your income. Table 14.1 outlines policies

Table 14.1   Overview of Insurance Needs.

Protection everyone needs	Protection dependent on what you own	Protection if someone relies on your income
• Health Insurance • Disability Insurance • Property Insurance	• Auto Insurance • Umbrella/Liability Insurance	• Life Insurance

that everyone should have, policies that are dependent on what you own, and policies you should have if others rely on your income.

Regardless of the type of insurance policy, you'll want to pay attention to two interconnected terms, which appear across insurance policies:

- **Premium**: The cost you pay for an insurance policy, often on a monthly or annual basis.
- **Deductible**: An amount of money you pay out-of-pocket before your insurance policy begins covering payments.

Generally, *policies with higher deductibles will have lower premiums*. As you consider the appropriate deductible amount for a particular insurance policy, you should weigh the monthly savings from a higher deductible compared with the higher potential outlay required when you make a claim. Regardless of the deductible amount you choose, you'll want to ensure you have enough money set aside in an emergency fund to be able to cover that amount.

Using Table 14.1 as a roadmap, let's now review the various types of insurance policies that you should consider enrolling in if you don't have them already.

Protection Everyone Needs

Health Insurance

Picking a health insurance policy is a confusing and stressful experience for most of us. Personally, I'd rank it up there with assembling furniture or trying to figure out how to fix anything in my apartment. But enrolling in the right health plan can save you a great deal of money and even affect the quality of your medical care, so it's important to make your decision carefully.

Most Americans can choose from a variety of health insurance policies, which primarily differ based on their flexibility in coverage and associated costs.

Flexibility in Coverage

Two main factors determine the level of flexibility of your health insurance coverage: 1) the doctors you can see, and 2) whether you need a referral from a primary care physician to visit a specialist.

Health care providers are usually categorized into two buckets — in-network and out-of-network. Doctors that have contracts or relationships with a particular insurance company are considered "in-network," and all other doctors are considered "out-of-network." Plans also differ based on whether you need a referral from a primary care physician to see a specialist who focuses on a particular area of medicine, such as an endocrinologist, allergist, or dermatologist.

What You Pay

Health plan costs differ based on what you pay upfront before coverage kicks in (i.e., deductibles), what you pay on an ongoing basis for care (i.e., monthly premiums, copayments, co-insurance), and how much in total you may have to pay in a year (i.e., out-of-pocket maximums).

When you choose a plan with less flexibility, you may be able to pay lower overall costs for your health care.[2] On the other hand, if you require more flexibility in your health care options, you may pay higher upfront and ongoing costs for that optionality.

How to Decide

Most US consumers covered by an employer plan are enrolled in one of five types of health insurance policies:

- Health Maintenance Organization (HMO) plans
- Exclusive Provider Organization (EPO) plans
- Preferred Provider Organization (PPO) plans
- Point-of-Service (POS) plans
- High Deductible Health Plan (HDHP) plans

Each policy type has its own advantages and disadvantages. For example, HMOs offer the least optionality among the various policy types because they only cover in-network medical care and require referrals for specialist visits. But on the plus side, they generally cost the least across the board. PPOs, which provide the most flexibility, cost the most for the average policyholder. And HDHPs charge the lowest premiums, but come with high deductibles and high out-of-pocket maximums. See Table 14.2 for a summary of flexibility of coverage by health plan.

When selecting a health plan, you're trying to balance flexibility and cost-effectiveness in a way that best accommodates your personal needs. While your exact health care plan options may vary, you'll want to ask yourself the following questions:

- *Do I need or want the flexibility to see out-of-network providers?*
  - If yes, consider a PPO, POS, or HDHP.
  - If not, you may want to save some money and consider an HMO, EPO, or HDHP.
- *Do I care about having to see a primary care physician before being able to see a specialist?*
  - If yes, consider an EPO, PPO, or HDHP.
  - If not, you may want to save some money and consider an HMO, POS, or HDHP.

I encourage you to run some numbers to figure out which plans available to you best align with how you use health care. Many

Table 14.2 Health Insurance Decision Matrix.

	In-network coverage only	In-network and out-of-network coverage
Referral Needed for Specialists	HMO	POS
No Referral Needed for Specialists	EPO	PPO

*HDHP could be structured as an HMO, EPO, PPO, or POS.

companies or their insurance providers have calculators you can use to model out different scenarios.

Disability Insurance

If you get sick or injured and are unable to work for a period of time, would you and your family be able to cover your living expenses? Disability insurance is meant to protect you against financial hardship in such a scenario — either on a short-term or long-term basis, depending on the policy type you're enrolled in.

Employer-Provided Coverage

If you work for a company, you likely already have some amount of employer-provided coverage. Employer-provided short-term disability policies typically last up to six months, and cover an average of 60% to 80% of your salary. Long-term disability kicks in after short-term coverage ends and could last up until your full social security retirement age (read: into your 60s). Long-term disability policies generally cover a lower percentage of your salary than short-term disability.

If you work for a company, be sure to verify your disability coverage and confirm the following before enrolling in a supplemental plan:

- **Coverage Amount**: What percentage of your salary does the company cover? Is the coverage based on your total salary (base, bonus, equity), or just your base salary?

- **Coverage Length**: When do short-term and long-term disability coverages begin and end, and how long could each last?
- **Elimination Period**: How long do you need to wait before your benefits kick in? (You can think of the elimination period as similar to a deductible, except instead of being based on some amount of spend, the elimination period is time-based.)
- **Pretax or Post-Tax Dollars**: Would your disability benefits be taxed? This is typically the case for employer-provided short-term disability; however, long-term disability benefits may not be taxed if you use after-tax dollars to pay for ongoing premiums.

  If you have a choice, pay for your long-term disability premiums with after-tax dollars rather than having the company pay the premiums. This will allow you to receive your disability benefits without being subject to federal income taxes, helping your benefits go toward your living expenses, rather than to the government.

Next, look back at the work you did in Chapters 4 and 5 to see what percentage of your salary you need to cover your daily living expenses. If the disability policies you receive through your employer provide a lower percentage than you need, you may want to explore supplemental disability policies while also examining whether you may have flexibility to decrease your living expenses, either now or in the event of a disability.

How to Choose a Disability Insurance Policy

When shopping for a long-term disability insurance policy, you'll want to confirm the following provisions:

- **Premium**: The amount you'll pay on a monthly or annual basis. While your premium will depend on the specific features of your policy, Policygenius estimates the yearly cost to be 1% to 3% of your annual salary in most cases.[3]

- **Benefit Amount**: The amount you'd receive each month if you needed to exercise your coverage.
- **Benefit Period**: The length of time you'd be able to receive benefits.
- **Elimination Period**: The amount of time you'd need to wait before your benefits kick in.
- **Disability Definition**: The terms dictating when you'd qualify as being disabled and be able to collect benefits, which typically fall into the categories "own occupation" and "any occupation." "Own occupation" means if you could not perform your particular occupation, you would be eligible for benefits, even if you could perform other occupations. "Any occupation" means you could not collect benefits unless you were unable to perform any "gainful occupation."

Property Insurance

Whether you rent or own your home, you need to have insurance to properly protect your personal belongings and home from fires, robberies, windstorms, and other not-so-fun events. Property insurance policies may differ in what they protect you from, so you'll want to examine the conditions of each option as you're shopping. For example, basic coverage generally excludes earthquakes and floods from its list of protections.

With that said, both renters and homeowners insurance provide coverage for:

- **Personal Belongings**: Insurance would protect most of your belongings, including your furniture, clothing, and electronics, but be sure to read the fine print because some policies may have limitations for jewelry, art, rugs, and tapestries, among others.
- **Additional Living Expenses**: If you were forced from your home because of a *covered* disaster, insurance would pay for the additional costs you'd incur while your home was being repaired, including hotel bills and restaurant expenses. However, note that not all disasters are considered "covered" disasters, such as a bed bug infestation.

- **Liability Insurance**: Insurance would protect you if someone were injured on your property, or you were sued for damaging another person's property.

Homeowners insurance includes the additional coverage of:

- **Dwelling**: Homeowners insurance would protect your home, garages, and sheds if damaged in certain events.

Replacement Cost versus Actual Cash Value

When seeking out either type of property insurance, you'll be able to get coverage based on the actual cash value or replacement cost of your personal property and housing. Most homeowners insurance policies will cover the structure of your home (i.e., the "dwelling" portion of your plan) based on replacement cost, and your personal property coverage will be limited to some percentage of your dwelling coverage, typically 50% to 70% according to the Insurance Information Institute.[4] Erik Chiprich, an insurance agent at State Farm Insurance, notes that in his 10 years in the business, he has never sold a homeowners insurance policy based on actual cash value. With that said, it's always good to confirm the type of coverage you're purchasing.

The difference in coverage matters. Replacement cost coverage will reimburse you for the full cost to replace your property, while actual cash value coverage will take into account the age of the item and any wear and tear, and reimburse you for the full cost to replace your property, less depreciation. Another way to think about actual cash value is the amount someone would have been willing to pay for the item before the damage occurred.

To figure out the amount of personal property coverage you need, create an inventory of your belongings in a spreadsheet, along with an estimated value for each item. For your most significant items, such as furniture and electronics, take and keep photos of those items, and store them along with your inventory list using your preferred cloud storage provider. The pictures and inventory list will be helpful if you ever need to make a claim.

Why I Finally Decided to Get Renters Insurance

For many years, I didn't think renters insurance was worth it. The odds seemed pretty slim that an unfortunate event, like a natural disaster or robbery, would strike my home.

Then one day, I received a frantic knock on the door from my building superintendent. He immediately asked me, "Do you have running water spilling through your ceiling?"

What a bizarre question, I thought. I answered, "No, should I?"

The superintendent explained that a resident in the building had tried to take a bath that morning while the water supply had been turned off for a routine inspection. When no water came out, the resident forgot to switch the faucet back to the "off" position and left his apartment to go to work. Later that afternoon, after the building had restored the water, the resident's bath overflowed. Not only did his apartment get flooded, but the surrounding apartments were also damaged.

I realized then and there that I needed renters insurance — which, for $10 to $20 a month, would not only protect my personal belongings against unlikely events, but also other people's everyday actions.

Protection Dependent on What You Own

Auto Insurance

If you own a car, you're required to have car insurance, which helps to protect against damage *to* your car and *because of* your car. Each state has its own minimum requirements for auto insurance policies, which may include coverage involving 1) liability insurance,

2) personal injury protection, and 3) uninsured or underinsured motorist coverage.

It's important to understand each component of your auto insurance policy and whether your current coverage is adequate based on your personal situation. For certain types of coverage, such as personal injury protection, the state minimum coverage may be sufficient, especially if you have existing health and disability insurance. On the other hand, if you have significant assets, the minimum required liability insurance may not be enough for your situation.

As with other insurance policies, you'll want to balance monthly premiums with when your coverage kicks in. Your monthly premium will decrease as you increase the amount of your deductible.

Umbrella/Liability Insurance

While you may have some liability insurance coverage through your property and/or auto insurance, it may not be sufficient to cover large claims and fully protect your financial assets. That's where an umbrella policy comes in.

An umbrella policy provides you with additional liability insurance above and beyond coverage from other insurance. For example, let's say you caused a car accident and you were on the hook for a $1 million claim for bodily injuries and the other driver's lost wages from being unable to work. Unfortunately, your auto insurance policy only covers the other driver up to $400,000. Having an umbrella policy would help fill the $600,000 gap, protecting your hard-earned savings from being depleted.

Umbrella policies are typically sold in $1 million increments with minimum coverage of $1 million. For the amount of coverage you get, these policies are pretty affordable. A $1 million policy may set you back just $100 to $300 a year. The rule of thumb is to choose an umbrella policy sufficient to shield your net worth. I'd recommend evaluating your coverage at least once a year to ensure you increase your umbrella policy coverage as your net worth grows.

Protection If Someone Depends on Your Income

Life Insurance

Life insurance provides a safety net so that people who rely on your income could support themselves and pay for their living expenses in the event of your death. Getting a life insurance policy is a must if anyone depends on you financially, including a partner, children, or other family members. If you have substantial assets that may be sufficient to support your dependents after you're gone, you may not need life insurance.

Those who work for a company are probably already enrolled in an employer-sponsored life insurance policy. Company life insurance policies often offer at least $50,000 of coverage, with the option to add coverage above that amount based on your salary or total compensation. There are a few catches, though: the amount of coverage you're able to secure may not be sufficient for your needs, and once you leave the company, you may or may not be able to take the policy with you.[5] In the cases where you are able to port or convert your coverage into an individual policy, the amount of your coverage and your premium could be significantly different (translation: much higher), depending on the coverage type, your age, and health status, among other factors. So if someone else counts on your salary and you are not independently wealthy, it may make sense to buy a life insurance policy that is not tied to your employer, especially if your path to reaching retirement or financial independence is still a number of years away.

Term Life versus Permanent Life

Life insurance policies generally fall into two main buckets: term life and permanent life. Term insurance works by insuring your life for a temporary period of time, typically 1 to 30 years. If you were to pass away during this time, the insurance company would pay the amount of the death benefit to your beneficiary. Let's say you enrolled in a 20-year term life policy with a death benefit of $1 million. If you passed away at any time during the next 20 years, your beneficiary would receive $1 million. However, your beneficiary wouldn't receive a penny if you passed away after 20 years.

Permanent life insurance, on the other hand, is more permanent and covers you for your whole life, hence the name. In addition to providing a death benefit, permanent life insurance also has an investment component, known as cash value, which builds over time and can be borrowed against. There are many variations of permanent life insurance, including traditional whole life, universal life, variable life, and variable universal life.

When deciding whether to get term or some form of permanent life insurance, you should consider the following factors:

- **Is my need temporary or permanent?** If you're like most people, you may only have a temporary need for life insurance to enable your dependents to pay off the mortgage and/or replace your income for some period of time. In those cases, it may make sense to simply push forward with a term life policy. In certain cases, if your need for life insurance is greater than 30 years or you have a unique tax and planning situation, then a permanent life policy may make sense to explore.
- **How long will I need the policy?** If your need is temporary and you're targeting a term life policy, the answer to this question should reflect how long you need to protect your income for your beneficiaries. Families with young children typically choose to take out policies that will protect them through when their last child finishes college. Others may choose to protect their income stream through their target retirement date, at which point, any dependents will have likely saved enough money to cover their living expenses.
- **How much of a benefit do my survivors need?** The size of the benefit should reflect: a) the living expenses of your surviving beneficiaries, 2) how long they will need to cover those expenses, and 3) any other major expenses or savings goals they will need to fund.

Table 14.3   Estimating Life Insurance Needs.

Ongoing Needs	
(1) Annual Income Needed	
(2) Annual Income of Survivor	
(3) Annual Income to Fund (1–2)	
(4) Number of Years to Replace Income	
(5) Total Ongoing Needs to Replace (3x4)	
Upfront Needs	
(6) Funeral Expenses	
(7) Mortgage Balance to Pay	
(8) Non-Mortgage Debt to Pay	
(9) College Funding and Other Unfunded Needs	
(10) Other Upfront Needs	
(11) Total Upfront Needs to Fund (6+7+8+9+10)	
(12) Estimated Life Insurance Needed (5+11)	

Table 14.3 incorporates these three variables to help you estimate the amount of life insurance you may need (also available at www.workyourmoneybook.com). When inputting the numbers for your situation, confirm you are not double counting expenses by including the same expense in your ongoing and upfront needs. For example, if you allocate money to pay off your entire mortgage, make sure to subtract the monthly mortgage payment from the annual income needed. Lastly, be sure to confirm this calculation with a financial professional before taking out a policy.

- **Do I need an investment component to my policy?** Term life is pure insurance, while a permanent life policy combines life insurance and an investment component. If you plan to follow the savings and investment guidance presented in earlier chapters, then you may not need an investment component with your insurance. However, if you need a forcing function to get you to save money, the investment component of a permanent life policy could serve in that capacity.

- **How much can I afford?** Regardless of what policy may be the best fit for your needs, cost may end up being the deciding factor. According to NerdWallet, a 30-year-old male may pay $9,283 a year for a $1 million whole life policy (a type of permanent insurance), but just $657 a year for a $1 million, 30-year term life policy — making the whole life policy 14 times more expensive in this example.[6] In addition to being more expensive, some people may simply not have an extra $9,000 (or whatever the larger amount is) lying around to divert to a permanent life policy.

While there are certainly some cases where getting a permanent life policy may make sense, a term policy is typically sufficient for most people. David Oransky, financial planner at Laminar Wealth, says, "I have yet to recommend permanent life insurance to any of my clients. For nearly everyone, they would be better off taking out a term life policy and investing the difference."

Estate Planning

Estate planning allows you to create a plan for your assets and your loved ones in the event that you pass away or are incapacitated, rather than leaving it to what state law dictates or the whim of a judge. In particular, you can make sure your assets are transferred to the right people, and designate trusted friends or relatives to care for your children and pets in the case of your passing. You can also identify people to make financial and health care decisions on your behalf in the scenario that you are living, but incapacitated.

"So much can – and does – go wrong when someone passes away or becomes incapacitated," says New York estate planning attorney Anthony Ford. "Estate planning is a means of proactively caring for family and loved ones, ensuring they are properly provided for and not saddled with legal burdens and difficult decisions that breed family conflict."

Regardless of your age, health, or net worth, it's important to take some time to think through your estate plans. With that said, the extent of the estate planning needed will depend on your particular situation and circumstances. A recent college graduate with little to no assets may not need a will to spell out that her Winnie the Pooh collection should go to her parents in case she passes away. On the other hand, a married couple with kids may require more comprehensive planning to make sure their loved ones are taken care of in their absence.

Let's walk through the main tools used for estate planning, which include wills, health care proxies and living wills, and powers of attorney.

Wills

All of us are familiar with the concept of a will. Wills allow you to control who would receive your stuff if you were to pass away, like the money in your checking and taxable brokerage accounts, as well as your espresso machine, that fancy Herman Miller desk chair, and your five-year-old futon.

Wills also enable you to determine who would serve as a guardian for any children and pets you have, and to establish trusts for those you care about, including minor children. By creating a trust for minor children, you can avoid two unfavorable situations – your children receiving a large inheritance outright when they turn 18 and having the state become the guardian of your assets in the event that both you and your partner died.

Lastly, you'll also name an executor – someone you trust who will be responsible for carrying out the instructions in your will.

Health Care Proxies and Living Wills

Health care proxies and living wills are estate planning tools that you can use to help ensure that medical decisions are carried out for you in a particular way if you were unable to communicate or make them yourself. Specifically, a health care proxy allows you to spell out *who* would make medical decisions for you, while a living will allows you to spell out *what* medical decisions you would want in various circumstances. You could choose to have both a health care proxy and a living will, or only one.

If you plan on working with an estate planning lawyer, seek their advice regarding which health care planning options would make the most sense for you. If your situation requires minimal estate planning, you may be able to use standard online forms (most states offer these) to complete your health care proxy and living will.

Power of Attorney

There's no escaping the bills we pay – even in the tragic event of a medical emergency. A power of attorney allows you to determine who would take care of those financial matters for you if you were unable to do so. You can authorize this person (or people) to carry out a range of actions on your behalf, such as selling property, signing legal documents, closing or opening accounts, or executing business transactions.

Other Ways to Transfer Your Assets

While wills are a key tool you can use to transfer your assets to the right people, they aren't the *only* tool available. In fact, wills can be less advantageous than other estate planning vehicles because they are subject to probate – a legal process used to validate a will, pay any remaining liabilities of an estate, and properly distribute one's assets. Going through probate can add costs and may delay when your beneficiaries receive your assets for up to a year or longer (depending on your state).

Given the potential expenses and inefficiencies of transferring assets through wills, you might want to consider using beneficiary designations and joint titling of your accounts and property, and in certain cases, living trusts as alternative estate planning vehicles that would allow you to bypass probate – either completely or partially.

Beneficiary Designations

Many accounts allow you to designate a beneficiary, who would inherit your account if you were to pass away without the estate first needing to go through probate. Accounts with beneficiary designations include:

- **Retirement Accounts and Life Insurance**: You can use beneficiary forms to denote a beneficiary for retirement accounts (e.g., 401(k)s, 403(b)s, IRAs), life insurance policies, annuities, and education savings accounts (e.g., 529 plans).
- **Transfer-on-death Accounts**: Beneficiaries can be added to bank and brokerage accounts as well. A bank account with a beneficiary is known as a payable-on-death account, while a brokerage account with a beneficiary is called a transfer-on-death account.

Financial Hygiene Tip

Check your beneficiary designations annually to ensure they are up to date.

Titling of Accounts and Property

Certain joint titling of accounts or property[7] allow those assets to pass outside of probate, including titling accounts or property as joint tenants with right of survivorship (JTWROS) or tenants by the entirety. In both cases, if one owner passes away, all of the assets would pass to the other owner without going through probate. Tenants by the entirety works in the same way as JTWROS, except tenants by the entirety is only available in certain states and for married couples.

Living Trusts

Living trusts allow you to specify exactly how your assets should be distributed after your passing without the cost and hassle of probate. As an added benefit, living trusts enable the details of your estate to remain private. That's the good news.

The downside? Establishing a living trust requires extra legwork and more upfront costs that may be unnecessary for some people. According to Ford, "For many people – particularly young professionals and married couples – there are easier ways to avoid probate, like using joint titling and beneficiary designations."

However, a living trust could be helpful in certain scenarios. For example, people who own real estate in more than one state and whose estate may otherwise be subject to probate proceedings in several states might use a living will to avoid this situation. If you're considering a living trust, I'd recommend consulting with an estate planning lawyer first to understand the pros and cons for your situation.

That Wasn't So Bad, Was It?

Congratulations: you've educated yourself on the dreaded topics of insurance and estate planning! Based on everything you've learned, you are ready to take the following steps to protect your wealth.

- Review your existing insurance policies to confirm the coverage aligns with what you need. Revise these policies as needed, including by adjusting deductibles or changing health plans, to better align with your situation.
- Make a list of insurance policies that you don't have, but need. Research each of these policies, contact insurance professionals to learn about the key provisions and secure price quotes, and then get yourself protected.
- Confirm your beneficiary designations and titling of accounts are correct, and consider setting up a recurring calendar event to revisit these items once a year.
- If you don't have a will, health care proxy and living will, and power of attorney already, you might want to speak with an estate planning attorney to understand your needs and the cost of drafting up a plan.

Part V

How to Stay the Course and Enjoy the Journey

"To be nobody but yourself in a world doing its best to make you every-body else means to fight the hardest battle any human can ever fight and never stop fighting."

– E.E. Cummings

Now that you've tackled your career and money strategy (awe-some!), you might be thinking, "I've gotten what I wanted from this book, so can't I just get on with my life already?" But sit tight for just a little longer. These final chapters are packed with valuable information that could make the difference between whether or not you achieve the goals you've set.

As I'm sure you know from experience, even the best-laid plans can go awry. You'll inevitably be thrown some curveballs on the journey ahead that may make you stop and wonder if you've been thinking through things all wrong. I sure have. In this section, you'll arm yourself with tactics that will help you stay on track when the going gets tough, so that you can make sure that all the hard work you've done pays off.

One of the reasons why work and money decisions are so difficult is because they rarely have straightforward answers, and often involve real sacrifices. Should you leave a lucrative job for a better-fitting role, even though you're saddled with student debt? Should you cut back on traveling because you're trying to save, even though you might miss out on some great memories? Does it make sense to move to a lower-cost area so that you can achieve your financial goals, although that will mean being farther away from friends and family?

Because the right decision in these types of situations is so subjective, it can be tough to stay true to the priorities you've identified, especially if they go against traditional norms, or the opinions of the people you care about. You also might need to adjust your priorities as life circumstances change (and that's totally fine!). In the coming section, you'll learn what to do and who to call on for help when you experience moments of self-doubt. And then you'll be off to the races!

Chapter 15

Focus on What You Can Control and Tune out the Noise

If you've gotten this far, good for you! I thought I would have lost you slogging through insurance and estate planning. (That really *was* some intense stuff, right?)

But in all seriousness, great job. By now, you've probably begun formulating an action plan that will help you balance your professional and financial goals, which is an accomplishment in and of itself. However, as I'm sure you're already aware, goal-setting is only half the battle; actually staying the course can be the hardest part of all.

New Year's health and fitness resolutions are a prime example of how all of us can struggle to follow through on the objectives we set for ourselves. Every January, gyms are jam-packed with the regular gym rats, as well as all of the newbies who've resolved to get in shape. But by February, gyms have largely cleared out, leaving only the regulars behind.

To put it simply, change is tough. You have to switch up a routine that is familiar, even if it isn't perfect. And in the moment, the familiar might feel better than trying something different and adding new responsibilities to your plate. Besides, like most people, you probably feel like you don't have any time as it is. You might get especially discouraged if the messages you receive from your peers and loved ones run counter to your goals, or if you're struggling to balance your physical and mental wellness.

I totally get it. That's why this chapter will outline several strategies to help you follow through on your goals in a healthy, happy, and productive way. Then it'll nearly be go time!

Overcome the Fear of Failure

One of the most common obstacles to beginning a new path is the fear of failure. What if we start on a path and aren't able to accomplish what we intended? What's even the point of trying if it'll just be a waste of time? I remember battling these very thoughts initially after losing my job.

The following strategies can help you get more comfortable with failure, allowing you to move forward toward your goals and bounce back quickly when you face obstacles.

Get in the Right Mindset

In her book *Mindset*, Stanford University psychologist Dr. Carol Dweck explains that the way you view yourself can impact how you live your life – from the goals you set and the decisions you make to whether you can achieve what's important to you.[1]

Dweck's decades of research found that people think about their abilities with either a fixed or growth mindset. Those with fixed mindsets believe their skills, intelligence, and talents are set in stone. People with growth mindsets, on the other hand, believe they can build on and improve these characteristics. Dweck also found that people's mindsets can vary by activity. For example, someone could have a fixed mindset when it comes to math, but a growth mindset for sports.

Dweck says that people are most likely to succeed at a task with a growth mindset because they're apt to focus on growing and learning, rather than trying to prove themselves repeatedly. As she puts it, "The passion for stretching yourself and sticking to it, even (or especially) when it's not going well, is the hallmark of the growth mindset. This is the mindset that allows people to thrive during some of the most challenging times in their lives."

When I was younger, failing to achieve a goal would often damage my confidence and self-esteem – textbook signs of a fixed mindset. It wasn't until I lost my job in my late 20s that I began shifting toward a growth mindset. After stumbling upon Dweck's research, I realized that I had been thinking about my layoff as an absolutely terrible outcome, rather than seeing it as a learning opportunity that would help me eventually reach my goal of greater career satisfaction.

This simple discovery marked a turning point for me. With a growth mindset, I figured out that I could still apply and build on the analytical skills I had honed in investment banking, but within a different industry that better matched my desired lifestyle. Fortunately, I was able to find that combo when I began my new job at Google. My experience encouraged me to adopt an approach that has continued to keep me motivated when I face setbacks in life – including when it comes to optimizing my career and finances.

Diversify Your Identity

Another strategy for overcoming the fear of failure is diversification (read: not putting all your eggs in one basket) – a concept we touched upon earlier in relation to your career and investment strategies. But you can also diversify your very *identity* by taking purposeful steps to avoid defining your sense of self based on a single aspect of your life, such as your job title or the size of your checking account. In other words, diversifying your identity means valuing yourself for *all* the characteristics that make you you.

Tim Ferriss, technology investor and author of *The 4-Hour Workweek*, espouses the benefits to be gained from a diversified identity.

In one of his on-screen interviews, he explained, "When you have money, it's always smart to diversify your investments. That way if one of them goes south, you don't lose everything. It's also smart to diversify your identity, to invest your self-esteem and what you care about into a variety of different areas – business, social life, relationships, philanthropy, athletics – so that when one goes south, you're not completely screwed over and emotionally wrecked."[2]

I can relate to the picture that Ferriss paints. My mood was almost entirely dictated by how my job was going when I worked in finance. Sure, when I had a good day at work, I felt on top of the world, but if I happened to have a bad day, I'd quickly fall into a downward spiral. In more recent years, however, I've diversified my identity by starting a side hustle and prioritizing my family relationships. As a result, I've been able to avoid extreme emotional swings while becoming increasingly confident in my decisions across all facets of my life.

You, too, may find that a diversified identity helps you tune out messages of self-doubt that threaten to stand in the way of achieving your career and financial goals. And besides, it'll almost certainly make you happier – and who doesn't want that?

Don't Take Yourself Too Seriously

In the movie *Van Wilder*, the main character (played by Ryan Reynolds) provides the following advice to an incoming freshman student: "But you know what I've learned in my seven years at Coolidge ... Timmy? I've learned that you can't treat every situation as a life-and-death matter because you'll die a lot of times. Write that down."[3]

Like Timmy, I used to have a tendency to take life too seriously, especially where my job was concerned. Because I was insecure about my standing at work, I responded defensively to constructive feedback, overreacted when I made mistakes, and tried to cover up my weaknesses. Unsurprisingly, I wasn't on the top of everyone's list of picks when new projects or opportunities arose.

Fortunately, I discovered a mentor in my boss at Google who helped me realize the error of my ways. When I saw how he handled work situations with relative levity and ease, it dawned on me that I was making life overly difficult for myself. By mellowing out and seeing the lighter side of things, I've also discovered some unexpected benefits, like stronger connections with colleagues, greater stamina, and improved job performance. Best of all, I was able to build my resilience – a skill that has helped me stay true to my core career and financial goals, while opening me to opportunities for improvement.

When I asked Ramit Sethi, author of *I Will Teach You to Be Rich*, what one piece of advice he would give his 21-year-old self, he said, "I'd tell myself to loosen up and have more fun. When I look back, and when I was most rigid, I was less successful. The times when I was most flexible were when I was most successful, and that is true in relationships, finance, and careers."

Make Time

Time is something that a lot of us stress about: having enough of it, being able to manage it better, and not letting it slip away. So much so that Collective Soul, Hootie and the Blowfish, the Eagles, and Pink Floyd, among many other bands, have written songs about it.

The good news is, there are some easy ways to help you make better use of the time you have so that you can follow through on the goals you've set for yourself.

Do a Schedule Audit

Most of us have no idea how we spend our time – even if we *think* we do. In her book *168 Hours*, author Laura Vanderkam suggests people track their schedules in 15-minute increments for a week to understand what activities they're doing, and for how long.[4] Vanderkam says people are often surprised to discover how they actually spend their time. Once you do, you can identify opportunities to streamline your schedule, whether by changing the timing or frequency of certain activities, or completely eliminating them.

When I did this exercise myself, I realized I was wasting a lot of time between meetings that were spaced out by a couple of hours or less. Because those intervals weren't quite long enough for deep, strategic work, I'd often find myself surfing the web, perusing the Facebook updates of people I didn't care about, or online shopping, instead of being productive. So I decided to conduct an experiment of sorts and see what would happen if I instead bucketed similar activities together – for example, by scheduling all of my meetings back to back while blocking off several consecutive hours for strategic assignments each day.

The experiment worked even better than I had hoped. Not only did my new approach help me decrease the amount of wasted time between activities, but it also reduced the switching costs that I had been incurring by reorienting myself between different types of tasks. I encourage you to try bucketing similar activities yourself. If your experience is anything like mine, you might be amazed to discover how much more time you gain, both at work and in your personal life.

Schedule Personal and Professional Activities in Your Calendar

Most of us use an online calendar application at work to help manage our commitments, including meetings and personal appointments. But I'd guess that very few of us are using calendars in the same way outside of our jobs. Maybe we should be.

Mike Steib, CEO of the online marketplace Artsy and author of *The Career Manifesto*, recommends using a calendar to schedule *all* parts of your day. "Block off every hour of your day in your calendar for something necessary or important to you, even sleeping, eating, and exercising," says Steib. "It may feel awkward at first, but over time, this system will change your life by helping you align your personal time with your true priorities, and making you more productive."

I've benefited from this strategy myself. In particular, I used to have a habit of letting my weekends escape me by watching the *Back to the Future* trilogy on repeat (yes, even *Back to the Future 3*). But when I began scheduling all of my activities into my calendar, I was able to stay on track with what I really wanted to be doing and reclaim my personal time. After a few weeks had passed, I could also reference my calendar to figure out what schedule worked best for me. For example, I found that mornings are the best time for me to work out, I need one to two hours to recharge after a big meeting or presentation, and I can't write for more than four hours at a time.

As an extra bonus, this strategy allows you to look back at how you spent your time for nostalgic purposes. While looking back at my schedule, I've been reminded of great dinners, nights out with friends, and some milestone events.

Make the Most of Mornings

I used to look forward to sleeping in on the weekends. After a long week of classes or work, I felt like I deserved the chance to snooze until 11 a.m. Not anymore. After auditing my schedule and calendaring my personal and professional commitments, I discovered that mornings are often a goldmine for me to complete tough tasks.

Scott Miller, Executive Vice President of Business Development and Chief Marketing Officer at FranklinCovey, says he's always been a morning person, but recently changed how he thought about his mornings. He explains, "Instead of just being productive in the mornings, I'm beginning to think about not just *how much* I can accomplish, but specifically *what* I should accomplish. I think about what activity, if completed early in my day, would make me more productive, less stressed, and more relaxed for the remainder of the day. As you can imagine, the answer is often tackling a hard task, or something I've been avoiding."

But you don't have to be a natural early bird like Miller to maximize the morning hours. Think about how you currently spend this time and what you may be able to achieve instead if you restructured your schedule. Then give it a go! You very well might discover that you're able to accomplish more during the mornings than any other time of day because you're refreshed from a night of sleep and lack the distractions that naturally arise during work hours.

Handle Other People

Other people can have a big impact on what we do or don't do with our lives, the way we spend our time and money, and how we feel about ourselves. And while you can't control the actions other people take that may affect you, there are strategies you can use to control their impact on you and your goals.

Silence the Critics

Along your journey, you may face criticism from close friends or family or people you don't even know. I've certainly received my share of unwanted, and often unqualified, feedback – especially around some of my career decisions.

For example, when I decided to change industries after losing my job in banking, nearly everyone I knew had strong opinions that they couldn't resist sharing. Friends, family, and former colleagues often exclaimed, "Are you crazy? Why would you want to leave finance? Don't you like making good money?" Several people even declared, "There's no way you'll be able to transition to a career in tech – why would a tech company hire you?!"

People also gave me the third degree when I first launched a financial planning firm while working full-time at Google. "Why would you want to do that? Isn't that going to take a lot of time? And how much money can you even make from doing this?" they'd ask. Looking back, I realize that many of the comments were based on the person's limiting thoughts, or myths they believed about work and money. These ideas may have influenced how they lived their own lives – perhaps to the detriment of their happiness. But at the time, these subtle and not-so-subtle jabs would inflict me with self-doubt.

James Clear, author of the bestselling book *Atomic Habits*, recognizes the challenges of rebounding from criticism. He says, "A lot of times, criticism can be subtle, and someone may not even know they're criticizing you. When dealing with criticism, you're faced with the decision of whether you sacrifice the relationship or your goal. If a friend or family member is criticizing you, it's tough because both the relationship and goal matter."

But as I've seen for myself, critics are everywhere, so we need to be prepared for how to handle them in healthy and productive ways. Clear advises, "Depending on your comfort level, one strategy could be to simply use open communication. Another strategy, which could be used with people you know and strangers, is to praise the good and ignore the bad. When someone supports you, praise that person for it. When someone criticizes you, try to brush it off. Regardless of the source, focus on the road ahead rather than the criticism, and use those situations to recommit to your work and goals."

Personally, I've found the "praise the good and ignore the bad" strategy particularly effective. When my wife praises me for a job well done, I make sure to thank her for acknowledging my efforts. When she's critical of me for not emptying the dishwasher (hypothetically speaking, of course), I take a deep breath and try to just let that comment go. Praise the good, ignore the bad.

Combat Social Pressures

Social pressures are another inescapable part of life that can make us act against our true desires. Remember those days back in middle school when we draped ourselves in flannel shirts and baggy jeans, just because everyone else was doing it? That's the power of social pressure, my friend.

Because social pressures are so influential, we need to be very conscious about who we let into our lives. Or, as personal development expert and motivational speaker Jim Rohn puts it, "You are the average of the five people you spend the most time with."[5]

On that note, I encourage you to surround yourself with people or groups who share the goals you've set for yourself. For example, if you want to save more money, you might benefit from getting to know people who enjoy low-cost activities, like running or reading, instead of high rollers who insist on getting bottle service every weekend. By seeking out people with similar lifestyle choices, you will be less tempted to jump ship for the sake of social approval.

Going back to Rohn's comment, I suggest you take a moment and think about the five people you spend the most time with. Do you feel better or worse during and after you hang out with them? Do their interests and goals align or run counter to the life you want to live?

Stop Comparing Yourself to Others on Social Media

Social media can be a double-edged sword. On the one hand, it helps us to stay up to date on the lives of people we care about, keep tabs on old acquaintances, and even confirm that the randos who email us are in fact real people. On the other hand, though, it can trick us into wishing we had other people's digitally perfect lives.

It's a fact that the stories we follow on social media are misleading. In a 2012 study of more than 1,000 Swedish Facebook users, researchers found that participants were more likely to post positive updates about themselves than negative ones.[6] That makes sense – whether online or offline, we generally like to display ourselves in the best light possible. But the researchers warn that social media use can quickly turn into a comparison game, with unhealthy consequences for everyone involved. Their paper notes, "When Facebook users compare their own lives with others' seemingly more successful careers and happy relationships, they may feel that their own lives are less successful in comparison."

To combat this, Clear says, "Don't compare your full movie to someone else's highlight reel. Unless you want to change places with someone wholesale, it doesn't make sense to compare yourself to them. You may see a lawyer posting nice vacation pictures on social media, but what is not so apparent is the 80-hour work weeks they had to endure to pay for that trip. Clarify the trade-offs necessary and don't cherry pick successes from other people's lives, otherwise, you're just comparing apples to oranges."

My personal advice? Consider hiding status updates from anyone who isn't in your inner circle. Many social media platforms, including Facebook, allow you to do this without the other person knowing. This strategy allows you to enjoy the benefits of social media while sparing you the incessant feed of self-aggrandizing posts that may make you feel bad about yourself.

Feeling Good Along the Way

Even with all of the strategies we've discussed, it's natural to feel overwhelmed or off-balance from time to time while trying to execute your goals. Personally, when I get excited about a new idea or embark on a big project, it can very quickly become all-consuming – either out of excitement, stress, or most often both. But achieving your goals and maintaining your sanity don't have to be mutually exclusive. Here are some strategies that you can use to achieve the peace of mind you deserve.

Know When to Say No

I used to have a hard time saying no to people, especially at work. Like an obedient dog, I was quick to drop everything I was doing to fetch other people's stuff. "Can you do this last-minute assignment that is probably really tedious, and is due tomorrow morning?" Sure, sign me up! "Do you know where I can find this figure?" Absolutely, let me spend the entire day trying to track that down for you!

While it felt good to say yes in the moment and help other people out, doing so forced me to say no to working on more strategic projects, spending time with friends and family, and occasionally catching some needed R&R. You can probably see where this is going. Because I was so quick to say yes, I reached a point when other people's needs and agendas started to take precedence over my own – a dynamic that created significant and unnecessary stress for me.

The good news is that even "yes" people like me can reclaim their schedules. To do this, Miller recommends asking yourself multiple times a day whether what you're doing is the best use of your time – which, in a work setting, probably means doing tasks that meet the top needs of your clients and your organization. Miller reflects, "As I face this test multiple times a day, I'm becoming more courageous about saying no. It often means saying no to otherwise good projects, so I can say yes to something that could have an exponential impact on my learning, competence, or brand."

One could say that I've become a lot more catlike in recent years by following Miller's advice and exhibiting more independent thinking. In particular, I pause before responding to work requests and ask myself whether I'm best positioned to fulfill the task at hand, and what other assignments it will require me to put aside. This technique has allowed me to exert more control over my schedule, without losing sight of my company's big-picture priorities. Needless to say, I'm feeling a lot more Zen these days (relatively speaking).

Stay Mentally Fit

I'm sure you've had experiences when you didn't know if you could possibly manage to complete everything on your to-do list. For me, that was a typical Monday through Sunday in finance. In those situations, I'd usually jump to the conclusion that I'd have to work around the clock to get whatever I was working on across the finish line.

In retrospect, I realize that I probably could have been a lot more productive by periodically stepping away from my work, instead of always being on the go. I'm sure that 25-year-old Roger would have been skeptical of this approach, however. My response probably would have been something along the lines of: "What, take a break when I have so much stuff to do? In your dreams!"

Rachael O'Meara, author of *Pause*, recognizes the challenges of putting on the brakes when we're feeling overwhelmed – even though doing so could actually help us achieve our goals. She explains, "We often resist pausing because we think we will look like slackers, or we feel guilty about not charging forward in what we set out to do. In our always-on culture, especially in the western world and corporate life, we are rewarded for our never-ending to-do lists and our rapid pace."

O'Meara says that simply taking four 15-minute breaks a day can enhance your creativity, renew your spirits, and engage your senses. In particular, she says that shorter but more frequent breaks are more beneficial than long pauses if you want to boost your productivity.

In my own life, I've found that I can focus intently on a task for only so long. I often feel a lot less stressed by building in breaks to recharge and "just be" – whether that means writing in a journal, working out, being present while sipping a cup of coffee, or turning off my digital devices. Just remember: work will always wait for you, but peace and happiness require finding.

Help Yourself

In this chapter, you've learned about a number of strategies that can help you overcome internal and external obstacles to pursuing your work and money goals. It bears repeating that *all* of us will face setbacks on the path toward a more fulfilling life. But if you begin this journey knowing what tools you have at your disposal, you'll be able to rebound much faster.

While many of these approaches can be implemented quickly and on your own timetable, you may find yourself in a situation that you can't simply work through on your own. That's why in the next and final chapter, you'll learn about who you can turn to for guidance when you're facing particularly complex challenges or need reassurance. We've all been there – but as you'll see for yourself, sometimes a little help can go a long way.

Chapter 16

You Don't Have
to Do It Alone

Seeking Help from Others

I used to be *really* frugal during my 20s while working as a banker in New York City. Case in point: whenever summer rolled around, I would put a chilled wet towel on my neck to help me go to sleep rather than using air conditioning (until my girlfriend smacked some sense into me, that is). So as you can probably imagine, I wasn't about to shell out cash for professional advice when I was stressed about finding the right career path or managing my finances. Instead, I'd seek out the opinions of my friends and family – who weren't experts by any means, and whose advice might have actually hindered my progress.

While I was probably on the extreme side, I've seen a lot of people hesitate to work with service providers. Several of my financial planning clients have admitted that the reason they put off hiring a planner for so long was because they lacked confidence in the tangible benefit. I get where they're coming from. If you want to buy a television, you can go to the store and see exactly what you'd be getting for your money before spending a dime (plus, there's usually some sort of return policy). But when it comes to services that are less concrete, such as career or financial advice, you have no guarantee of a particular outcome.

Clearly, though, I've come around on this issue – to the point that I'm now a service provider myself! The truth is, I've learned through firsthand experience that we all need help sometimes. So if you do find yourself struggling to achieve your career and financial goals, I'd encourage you to consider calling in a pro. And even if you believe you've created a rock-solid action plan for yourself, it might still make a lot of sense to consult with an expert. In fact, I'd argue that nearly everyone can benefit from professional advice once in a while.

In this chapter, we'll explore whether engaging a service provider might make sense for your situation, the types of providers out there, and how to choose one.

What Service Providers Offer

A lot of people question whether working with a service provider is worth it. Unfortunately, I can't give you a definitive answer. All of us define "worth it" in different ways. But certainly, service providers offer a number of important benefits that you can't get on your own. Let's consider the advantages, shall we?

You Might Get Answers Faster

Professionals can often help you answer complex questions with remarkable efficiency because they have encountered similar situations many times before. While they may not be able to tell you exactly what to do since that reflects your preferences and priorities, their advice can help short-circuit the decision-making process.

You'll Get an Unbiased Point of View

Let's get real: it's tough to give objective advice to people we care about. For example, your parents may encourage you to go into a particular field because it would make them proud, although it may not necessarily be the best fit for your desired lifestyle. Or your friends might encourage you to save up to buy a house because they want you to stay in the area, but they haven't considered your other financial goals. Because professionals are emotionally removed from your situation, they are generally better positioned to provide unbiased guidance that will help you get where you want to go.

You Can Avoid Blind Spots

It wasn't until after I became a Certified Financial Planner and had been working with planning clients for some time that my wife and I decided we should hire a financial planner ourselves. While I've gained a great deal of knowledge through my training, I don't know everything. I recognize that enlisting a professional can help ensure I'm not overlooking an important detail, even when it comes to my own field.

Who You Can Call

There are a number of different types of service providers that can help you achieve your personal goals. Some focus on your entire life; others focus on a specific area, such as your career or finances. Let's take a moment to learn about each type of service provider.

Career Coaches

While all career coaches help people improve one or more aspects of their careers, they can have different areas of expertise, techniques, and service offerings.

Career coaches may specialize in a particular industry, such as finance, technology, or marketing, or a specific situation, such as career exploration for recent college graduates, mid-career changes, or executive leadership training. Some coaches focus on the tactical aspects of a job search once you've already identified the type of work you're targeting; for example, they might help you polish up your resume and LinkedIn profile, guide you on how to find opportunities, provide interview tips, and assist with salary negotiation. Other coaches may primarily help you navigate the exploration phase by working with you to connect your interests and skills with possible jobs.

Nearly anyone can call themselves a career coach because the title has no certification or licensing requirements. You may be able to find more qualified coaches by looking for those who have past experiences in recruiting or human resources functions, or who have attained certifications through organizations such as the International Coach Federation (ICF), the Professional Association of Résumé Writers & Career Coaches (PARW/CC), or the National Résumé Writers' Association (NRWA).

Financial Advisors and Planners

Like career coaches, financial advisors and planners can differ based on their areas of specialization, service offerings, and price structure.

Financial planners commonly work with a particular set of clients based on life phase or circumstance. For example, you can find planners who specialize in working with young professionals, new couples, retirees, divorcées, business owners, doctors, and teachers. Their services can include one-time sessions focused on answering your most pressing questions, comprehensive planning packages, and long-term engagements that include managing your investments on an ongoing basis.

The types of services a financial planner offers impacts the fee structure they use. In particular, financial planners who offer one-time sessions often charge by the hour, while planners who develop financial plans over one or more meetings typically charge a flat fee. Financial planners who work with clients on an ongoing basis have traditionally charged a fee based on the investment balance they're managing, known as an assets under management fee (AUM). However, a growing number of financial planners are now offering these services for a flat recurring monthly fee instead that may be based on the amount of your income or net worth, or the complexity of your financial situation.

While the requirements to become a financial planner are minimal, you may come across planners who have achieved certain designations, such as Certified Financial Planner (CFP), Certified Public Accountant (CPA), or Chartered Financial Analyst (CFA), which could give you clues into a provider's expertise. CFPs usually provide guidance on several aspects of a client's financial situation, while CPAs have a particular focus on taxes and CFAs have an expertise in investment management.

Life Coaches and Therapists

If you're looking for assistance with broader life topics, life coaches and therapists may be a helpful resource.

Caitlin Magidson, who works as both a career and life coach and a licensed therapist, explains, "While both types of providers focus on helping people achieve greater happiness and emotional stability, they typically use different approaches. Life coaches often serve as a motivating force by helping you create an action plan for a specific goal, and then monitoring your progress. Therapists, on the other hand, can work with you to process emotions, understand behaviors and thoughts that come up associated with past or current experiences that are preventing you from pursuing your goals."

Life coaches and therapists also have different licensing requirements. Similar to career coaches, life coaches do not have to have a master's-degree-level training or licensure, although some choose to attain a coaching certification through ICF-approved or ICF-accredited programs. The licensing requirements for therapists are more stringent, and include a bachelor's degree, a master's degree, and a certain number of hours of supervised therapy.

According to Magidson, both coaches and therapists may be able to help you with a specific personal issue, or they can work with you more broadly on topics related to your future life direction and purpose. For example, some coaches focus on relationships and love, while others may focus on your finances. Similarly, some therapists run general practices treating anxiety and depression, while others specialize in a specific area, such as trauma, grief and loss, or relationships, or specific populations, such as children, adults, couples, or families.

How to Save Money on Therapy

An advantage to working with a therapist is that unlike the other providers mentioned, your health insurance may cover some of your expenses, depending on your policy. So if you're seeking a therapist, consider reviewing Chapter 14, which covered how to pick the best health insurance plan for your needs. In most cases, you can use money from a health savings account or flexible spending account toward therapy expenses, which can help you decrease your taxable income (read: save you money). For further details about how this works, revisit Chapter 5.

How to Vet a Service Provider

The vetting process is neither easy nor scientific, but you should take the time to do it right since the provider you choose will be helping you address key aspects of your life. No matter what type of provider you're seeking, you'll want to consider the following factors to determine who the best fit might be.

Experience and Credentials

The amount of experience a service provider brings to the table will help shape your work together, with both newer and more seasoned professionals having their pros and cons. For example, newer practitioners may be more attentive and responsive, and less expensive.

However, they may not be able to leverage experiences from many other client situations and may not have dealt with your situation before. More experienced providers, on the other hand, will likely have seen a variety of client situations, which can benefit you. However, they may be more expensive and less responsive or accessible.

You should also review the provider's credentials, particularly if you're deciding between a life coach or therapist. Magidson explains, "I'd caution people to always check into a life coach or therapist's professional qualifications and education. A lot of people put up a shingle as a 'life coach,' but really have no training. I'd say when in doubt, it's better to go with a therapist who has more training if you are experiencing any mental health issues."

Expertise

You'll want to know if the provider you're considering specializes in a particular type of client or situation. For example, if you're in your 20s and seeking a financial planner, a provider who primarily works with retirees is probably not an ideal fit for either of you. Ask yourself: What makes this provider uniquely qualified to serve me?

Fit/Rapport

In most cases, you'll interact with the service provider via email, on the phone, and/or in-person before committing to work with them. In those initial interactions, ask yourself:

- Did we have a good rapport when we communicated?
- Would I actually look forward to meeting with this person, and likely for multiple sessions?
- Did I get a good vibe from this person?
- Do I feel like they understood me, that I could trust them, and that I'd feel comfortable sharing very personal details about myself with them?

Fees

Certainly, you'll also want to know how much the services will cost you. But beyond the basic numbers, you should also find out the following:

- How does the service provider charge (e.g., hourly fees, flat fees, or fees based on some other formula)? Most therapists charge hourly fees, while coaches (financial, life, career) charge hourly or flat fees. Financial planners generally charge hourly fees or flat fees, or based on a percentage of assets managed.
- Does the service provider receive compensation in other ways? For example, financial planners could get fees from clients only (i.e., fee-only), from clients and commissions (fee-based), or be paid on commission only.

Deliverables

You'll want to know what deliverables you'll actually receive for what you're paying. Deliverables may vary depending on service provider type. For example, therapists and certain life coaches may not be able to offer a straightforward or uniform deliverable because every client has different needs. Financial planners, however, typically offer clearer deliverables, such as a financial plan, ongoing supervision of your investment portfolio, and/or a certain number of check-in meetings throughout the year.

Bottom Line

Service providers can help you stay on your path, regardless of whether you need a little nudge to push forward with your action plan, want help maintaining your momentum, or would simply like to run your ideas by a professional.

For some people, deciding which type of service provider to enlist may be fairly obvious. Don't know how to invest your 401(k) or whether you can afford to buy a house in five years? Go to a financial planner. Need help polishing up your resume and identifying opportunities when you've already decided to change jobs? See a career coach. In other cases, the decision is not so clear-cut. You may start by working with one type of service provider, only to realize through the process that you need help in a different area. For example, maybe you enlist a life coach to help you with your life direction, but through your work, you realize that a lot of your issues are stemming from past experiences that you need to confront. You may then engage a therapist to help you with those issues. Or perhaps through your work with a life coach, you've decided to start your own business and therefore need to hire a financial advisor to help you make the plan financially feasible.

But as someone once told me, regardless of your particular situation, you must have two things for a successful engagement with a service provider: courage and faith. You have to have the courage to admit you may need some outside help. And you have to have faith that the service provider will help you move closer to living the life you want.

Conclusion

I t's hard to believe that I started working on this book more than two years ago. At the time, I was writing a couple of personal finance articles a month for various publications – a workload that was pretty manageable. And so, I thought, writing a book couldn't be that much harder; I could simply crank out a couple more words per day, and I'd be finished by the end of the year. Well, that ended up being a huge miscalculation (long division was never my forte)!

In the end, though, I am glad I pushed myself to overcome the numerous setbacks I faced balancing this endeavor with my jobs and my personal life. What kept me going at first was a strong desire to share my experiences so that you and others might have an easier time navigating your career and finances, and that certainly remains the case.

But my motivations became a bit more personal when my wife and I found out we were expecting a baby shortly after securing the book deal. And so I embarked on this project with my future son, Owen, at the forefront of my mind. In particular, I wanted to write a book that aggregated all the career and money lessons I hoped to teach Owen, who arrived into the world just a few days after I completed my first draft.

This book was a long time coming. My professional and financial challenges felt like a black cloud over my head for most of my 20s, eventually throwing me into a state of panic when I lost my job. I desperately sought answers and relief by reading countless books and articles, and even becoming a Certified Financial Planner. But it didn't have to be that hard.

My hope for you and Owen is that by being deliberate about your finances early and consistently, you can accumulate the financial runway you need to find a meaningful career, achieve your financial goals, and live a satisfying life. If you get nothing else from the book, I want you to remember four takeaways.

Don't Limit What You Can Do

Don't let the career myths that we discussed in Chapter 2, or other people's limiting thoughts, prevent you from designing the life that you want.

I'm in no way saying everyone can become an astronaut or the CEO of a Fortune 500 company. But I also don't think you need to "kill it" at work or "work yourself to death" to achieve financial freedom and live a fulfilling life. You have plenty of levers at your disposal – don't artificially limit what you can do.

Get Comfortable with Being Uncomfortable

When I was interviewing for summer internships in college, my career counselor and several professors recommended I come prepared with a 5-year and 10-year career plan. Looking back, I realize that was one of the worst pieces of advice I've ever received. The truth is, no one knows how their life will unfold over the next several months, let alone the next 5 to 10 years.

Creating a rigid plan may provide you with a false sense of certainty that doesn't really exist, and it may also cause you unnecessary guilt if you ever do stray from your carefully plotted path.

Instead, my advice is to understand your preferences and values in your work and life, along with the trade-offs you're willing to make. Use those guiding principles to determine what opportunities you decide to explore and take, and which ones you'll gladly turn down. Knowing what you want and what's important to you will serve you much better in the long run than some made-up five-year plan.

Know That Money Won't Make You a Better Person

In the book *The Art of Living*, author Bob Proctor says, "Money doesn't make you a better person, it makes you more of what you already are. If you're not a nice person, you'll become unbearable. If you are a nice person, you'll become a nicer person."[1]

The point is, don't prioritize accumulating money at the expense of everything else you care about. In real life, people don't suddenly turn the ship around and become a good person once they've "made it." Instead, try to be your best self every day – treat people with kindness, give others the benefit of the doubt, tip generously, admit when you're wrong, and forgive easily. When you exude positivity, you are more likely to identify and attract new opportunities that will help you achieve your goals – whether professionally, financially, or personally. It turns out that money might not make you a better person, but being a better person will get you more in life than money ever could.

Start Now

As luck would have it, getting laid off a few months before my 30th birthday turned out to be one of the best things that's ever happened to me. In losing my job, I gained the time and space to think about how I really wanted to live – an experience that changed the course of my life for the better.

It didn't take me long to realize that a lot of my uncertainties centered on how I could navigate work and money to maximize my happiness. Until then, I had never reflected on my career or financial choices, even though these topics caused me considerable worry. Now out of a job and looking to transition industries, the question looming in my mind was: how could I find work I loved, without sacrificing my financial and lifestyle goals (or my sanity, for that matter)?

In the end, I was able to find career satisfaction *and* financial security using the strategies in this book. But just imagine if I had started earlier. Certainly, I could have accrued a lot more in savings by reaping the benefits of compound interest for longer. The additional financial runway might have even given me the ability to be choosier about my job.

But my biggest regret of all is the time that I lost. If I had done the work in this book in my early 20s, I could have achieved the goals I truly wanted, far sooner. Unfortunately, I'll never be able to reclaim the years I squandered chasing the wrong things in life. Maybe you can learn from my mistakes.

A Final Word

The plan you've been developing over the course of this book required you to take an honest look at yourself, including understanding your values and how the different pieces of your life fit together and impact each other. You delved into the fundamentals of career planning and personal finance, while applying that knowledge to your own life. I've challenged you to think through tough questions, crunch some numbers, and remain committed for the long haul. But the hardest part is behind you.

Your self-reflection and willingness to revisit your past decisions should give you the confidence that you're moving toward the life you want. In particular, the insights you've gained will help you achieve your goals, even as they continue to evolve. The best part is that once you begin implementing your action plan, you can spend your days doing more of what you want to do, and less time worrying.

Congratulations on a job well done. Now go off and work your money, and enjoy your life.

Acknowledgments

Writing a book is a big undertaking – even bigger than I initially thought. The time I spent researching, writing, editing, and obsessing about this project meant I had less availability for a host of other activities, like watching TV, hanging out with friends and family, or just "being" – and that had a disproportionate impact on one person in my life.

So first and foremost, thank you to my wife, Jennifer. Throughout our time together, your love, support, and encouragement have given me the confidence and safety to do things I never thought would be possible — including, broadly speaking, to design a life on my terms, and in this instance, to write a book. I've told you this many times, but I *literally* could not have done this without you. You continue to make me a better person and a better writer. And for the book, you took the time to talk through ideas (some that were very bad), review drafts (many that were painful to read), and edit what sounded okay (that's being generous) into content that a reader may enjoy reading. And just as importantly, you kept me sane along the way.

Early in this process, I learned that traditional publishers typically will not consider publishing your work unless you come through a literary agent who has vetted you and your book idea. Each agent and editor receives hundreds, if not thousands, of book proposals from prospective writers a year, which means they have to turn down *a lot* of writers. I'm thankful to my literary agent, Linda Konner, and my editor, Kevin Harreld, for believing in me and my book, understanding my vision, and championing this project.

Many people have helped bring this book to fruition by generously supporting my financial planning and writing pursuits over the years. I am particularly grateful to personal finance expert Lauren Lyons Cole, who helped me initially get my business off the ground by advising me on ways to build my writing portfolio and financial planning firm. Several other subject matter experts helped me when it came to writing this book specifically. Financial planner David Oransky served as my sounding board for the finance section, insurance agent Erik Chiprich and estate planning attorney Tony Ford assisted with the insurance and estate planning chapter, and career management expert Amanda Augustine provided invaluable input on the career section. A number of my friends also reviewed and provided feedback on my early drafts, including Steffi de Zarraga, Veena Ramaswamy, Elizabeth Bouquard, Aman Randhawa, Gouri Mukherjee, Alberto Grazi, Amanda Blake, and Serenity Hughes. And of course, I'm fortunate for the continued support I have received from the rest of my friends and my family.

Finally, I'd like to thank my parents for all the work they put into raising me. Before becoming a parent, it was not apparent to me how much work and sacrifice are required to bring up any child, let alone a high-energy, rebellious kid like I was. So thank you, Mom and Dad, for keeping me on track.

– Roger Ma

Endnotes

Part 1: Here's the Deal

Chapter 1: You're Worth More Than You Think

1. Anna Robaton, "Why So Many Americans Hate Their Jobs," CBS News, March 31, 2017, https://www.cbsnews.com/news/why-so-many-americans-hate-their-jobs/

2. Jean Chatzky, "65 Percent of Americans Are Losing Sleep Over Money. Here's How to Change it," NBC News, December 19, 2017, https://www.nbcnews.com/better/business/65-percent-americans-are-losing-sleep-over-money-here-s-ncna831096

3. Blair Decembrele, "Encountering a Quarter-life Crisis? You're Not Alone...," LinkedIn Official Blog, November 15, 2017, https://blog.linkedin.com/2017/november/15/encountering-a-quarter-life-crisis-you-are-not-alone

4. *Fight Club*, film, directed by David Fincher, performed by Brad Pitt, Fox 2000 Pictures, Regency Enterprises, Linson Films, Atman Entertainment, Knickerbocker Films, Taurus Film, 1999.

5. Jennifer Ma, Matea Pender, and Meredith Welch, "Education Pays 2016: The Benefits of Higher Education for Individuals and Society," College Board, 2016, https://research.collegeboard.org/pdf/education-pays-2016-full-report.pdf

6. Seattle Times staff, "A Brief History of Retirement: It's a Modern Idea," *Seattle Times*, December 31, 2013, https://www.seattletimes.com/nation-world/a-brief-history-of-retirement-its-a-modern-idea/

7. "2019 Retirement Confidence Survey Summary Report," Employee Benefit Research Institute and Greenwald & Associates, April 23, 2019, https://www.ebri.org/docs/default-source/rcs/2019-rcs/2019-rcs-short-report.pdf

8. "Life Expectancy at Birth, Female (Years) – United States," World Bank, https://data.worldbank.org/indicator/SP.DYN.LE00.FE.IN?locations=US

9. William P. Bengen, "Determining Withdrawal Rates Using Historical Data," *Journal of Financial Planning*, October 1994, https://www.onefpa.org/journal/Documents/The%20Best%20of%2025%20Years%20Determining%20Withdrawal%20Rates%20Using%20Historical%20Data.pdf

10. Philip L. Cooley, Carl M. Hubbard, and Daniel T. Waltz, "Choosing a Withdrawal Rate That Is Sustainable," *AAII Journal*, February 1998, https://www.aaii.com/journal/article/retirement-savings-choosing-a-withdrawal-rate-that-is-sustainable

Chapter 2: Everything You've Been Taught About Jobs Is Wrong

1. Clay Christensen, *How Will You Measure Your Life* (Harper Business 2012), 36.

2. Abraham Maslow, "A Theory of Human Motivation," *Psychological Review*, 1943, http://psychclassics.yorku.ca/Maslow/motivation.htm

3. *Moneyball*, film, directed by Bennett Miller, performed by Brad Pitt, Columbia Pictures, Scott Rudin Productions, Michael De Luca Productions, Film Rites, Sidney Kimmel Entertainment, Specialty Films (II), 2011.

4. "Average Hours Employed People Spent Working on Days Worked by Day of Week," Bureau of Labor Statistics, 2018, https://www.bls.gov/charts/american-time-use/emp-by-ftpt-job-edu-h.htm

5. "Workplace Stress," American Institute of Stress, https://www.stress
.org/workplace-stress

6. Erik Sorenson, "Jack Welch and the Work-life Balance," CNBC, July 27,
2009, https://www.cnbc.com/id/32171152

Part 2: Figure Out Your Starting Point

Chapter 3: How's Your Job?

1. Amy Wrzesniewski and Jane E. Dutton, "Crafting a Job: Revisioning
Employees as Active Crafters of Their Work," Academy of Management
Review, April 2001, https://spinup-000d1a-wp-offload-media
.s3.amazonaws.com/faculty/wp-content/uploads/sites/6/
2019/06/Craftingajob_Revisioningemployees_000.pdf

Chapter 4: Compiling Your Financial Report Card

1. "What Is the Difference Between a Credit Report and a Credit Score?"
Consumer Financial Protection Bureau, August 3, 2017, https://www
.consumerfinance.gov/ask-cfpb/what-is-the-difference-
between-a-credit-report-and-a-credit-score-en-2069/

2. John Ulzheimer, "Can You Force Your Lender to Report Your Account to
the Credit Bureaus?" Mintlife Blog, December 26, 2011, https://blog
.mint.com/credit/can-you-force-your-lender-to-report-
your-account-to-the-credit-bureaus-122011/

3. "What's in My FICO Scores?" myFICO, https://www.myfico.com/
credit-education/whats-in-your-credit-score

4. "New Credit," myFICO, https://www.myfico.com/resources/
credit-education/credit-scores/new-credit

Chapter 5: How to Increase Your Financial Runway

1. "Consumer Expenditures –2018," Bureau of Labor Statistics, September
10, 2019, https://www.bls.gov/news.release/cesan.nr0.hTm

2. "IRS Provides Tax Inflation Adjustments for Tax year 2019," Internal Revenue Service, November 15, 2018, https://www.irs.gov/newsroom/

irs-provides-tax-inflation-adjustments-for-tax-year-
2019

3. Claire Bushey, "Script to Ask for a Lower Credit Card Rate," Credit-
   Cards.com, November 11, 2017, https://www.creditcards.com/
   credit-card-news/script-negotiate-better-credit-card-
   deal-1267.php

4. "Repayment Plans," FinAid, http://www.finaid.org/loans/repay
   ment.phtml#loanterm

Part 3: Optimize Your Job

Chapter 7: How to Tweak Your Job

1. Amy Wrzesniewski, Justin M. Berg, and Jane E. Dutton, "Turn the Job
   You Have into the Job You Want," *Harvard Business Review*, June 2010,
   https://spinup-000d1a-wp-offload-media.s3.amazonaws.com/
   faculty/wp-content/uploads/sites/6/2019/06/Turnthejobyou
   haveintothejobyouwant.pdf

Chapter 8: Supplement Your Job to Explore New Opportunities

1. Amanda Dixon, "The Average Side Hustler Earns Over $8k Annually,"
   Bankrate, June 25, 2018, https://www.bankrate.com/personal-
   finance/smart-money/side-hustles-survey-june-2018/

2. Patrick J. McGinnis, *The 10% Entrepreneur: Live Your Startup Dream Without Quitting Your Day Job* (Portfolio 2016), 43–45.

Chapter 9: Prepare to Change Your Job

1. "3 Habits That Could Increase Your Chances of Getting the Job," Indeed,
   https://www.indeed.com/career-advice/finding-a-job/3-
   habits-that-could-increase-your-chances-of-getting-the-
   job

2. Paul Wolfe, "Quality, Not Quantity: Why Employers Prefer Targeted
   Job Applications," Indeed Blog, October 24, 2017, http://blog
   .indeed.com/2017/10/24/why-employers-prefer-targeted-
   job-applications/

Chapter 10: Take Action to Change Your Job

1. "The Art of the Job Hunt," Randstad US, October 16, 2018, https://www
.randstadusa.com/jobs/career-resources/career-advice/
the-art-of-the-job-hunt/631/
2. "50 HR and Recruiting Stats that Make You Think," Glassdoor for Employers, https://b2b-assets.glassdoor.com/50-hr-and-recruit
ing-stats.pdf
3. Eric Ries, *The Lean Startup* (Currency, 2011), 101.
4. Will Evans, "You Have 6 Seconds to Make an Impression: How Recruiters See Your Resume," Ladders, March 12, 2012, https://www.theladders
.com/career-advice/you-only-get-6-seconds-of-fame-make-
it-count
5. Jon Shields, "Over 98% of Fortune 500 Companies Use Applicant Tracking Systems (ATS)," Jobscan Blog, June 20, 2018, https://www.jobscan
.co/blog/fortune-500-use-applicant-tracking-systems/

Part 4: Optimize Your Finances

Chapter 11: Chart Your Goals and How Much They Will Cost

1. *Full House*, TV series, directed by Joel Swick, performed by David Coulier, Jeff Franklin Productions, 1987-1995.

Chapter 12: What You Need to Know About Investing

1. *Back to the Future*, film, directed by Robert Zemeckis, performed by Michael J. Fox, Universal Pictures, Amblin Entertainment, and U-Drive Productions, 1985.
2. "Guide to the Markets: US, 2Q 2018," J.P Morgan Asset Management, March 31, 2018, https://www.wrapmanager.com/hubfs/blog-
files/JPMorgan%20Guide%20to%20the%20Markets%202Q%202018
.pdf
3. "Vanguard Portfolio Allocation Models," Vanguard, https://personal
.vanguard.com/us/insights/saving-investing/model-port
folio-allocations

4. "Guide to the Markets – US, 2Q 2018," J.P Morgan Asset Management, March 31, 2018, https://www.wrapmanager.com/hubfs/blog-files/JPMorgan%20Guide%20to%20the%20Markets%202Q%202018.pdf

5. GuruFocus, "The Powerful Chart That Made Peter Lynch 29% a Year for 13 Years," Forbes, June 26, 2013, https://www.forbes.com/sites/gurufocus/2013/06/26/the-powerful-chart-that-made-peter-lynch-29-a-year-for-13-years/#6020b0097bc0

6. Warren E. Buffett, "2018 Letter to the Shareholders of Berkshire Hathaway, Inc.," Berkshire Hathaway, February 23, 2019, https://www.berkshirehathaway.com/letters/2018ltr.pdf

7. Jeff Cox, "Global Economy Faces a 'Perfect Storm' in 2013: Roubini," CNBC, May 9, 2012, https://www.cnbc.com/id/47356500

8. Gary Kaminsky, "Time's Up Meredith Whitney, Muni Prediction Was Wrong," CNBC, September 27, 2011, https://www.cnbc.com/id/44670656

9. Mark Perry, "More Evidence That It's Hard to 'Beat the Market' Over Time, ~92% of Finance Professionals Can't Do It," American Enterprise Institute, March 19, 2019, https://www.aei.org/carpe-diem/more-evidence-that-its-really-hard-to-beat-the-market-over-time-92-of-finance-professionals-cant-do-it-2/

10. "401(k) Plan Fix-It Guide – 401(k) Plan – Overview," Internal Revenue Service, https://www.irs.gov/retirement-plans/401k-plan-fix-it-guide-401k-plan-overview

11. "FAQs – Auto Enrollment – What Is an Automatic Contribution Arrangement in a Retirement Plan?" Internal Revenue Service, https://www.irs.gov/retirement-plans/faqs-auto-enrollment-what-is-an-automatic-contribution-arrangement-in-a-retirement-plan

12. "Building Financial Futures," Fidelity Brokerage Services LLC, March 31, 2019, https://sponsor.fidelity.com/bin-public/06_PSW_Website/documents/BuildingFinancialFuturesQ12019.pdf

13. "Building Futures Q1 2019 Fact Sheet," Fidelity Investments Institutional Services Company, Inc., March 31, 2019, https://institutional.fidelity.com/app/literature/item/953591.html

14. "Financial Savings Report: The Real Cost of Fees," Personal Capital, 2015, https://static1.squarespace.com/static/56c237b2b09f95f2a778cab2/t/573b7492f699bbd9586c707d/1463514267850/PC_Fees_WhitePaper.pdf

15. Amie Tsang, "5 Pieces of Advice from John Bogle," *New York Times*, January 17, 2019, https://www.nytimes.com/2019/01/17/business/mutfund/john-bogle-vanguard-investment-advice.html

Chapter 13: How to Construct Your Portfolio

1. "Vanguard Target Retirement 2050 Fund," Vanguard, https://investor.vanguard.com/mutual-funds/profile/overview/vfifx
2. "Vanguard Target Retirement 2030 Fund," Vanguard, https://investor.vanguard.com/mutual-funds/profile/VTHRX
3. "Fidelity Freedom 2050 Fund," Fidelity, https://fundresearch.fidelity.com/mutual-funds/summary/315792416
4. "Fidelity Freedom Index 2050 Fund," Fidelity, https://fundresearch.fidelity.com/mutual-funds/summary/315793570

Chapter 14: Protecting Your Wealth

1. "Statistics and Facts," Brain Aneurysm Foundation, https://bafound.org/about-brain-aneurysms/brain-aneurysm-basics/brain-aneurysm-statistics-and-facts/
2. "HMO, POS, PPO, EPO and HDHP with HSA: What's the Difference?" Aetna, https://www.aetna.com/health-guide/hmo-pos-ppo-hdhp-whats-the-difference.html
3. Colin Lalley, "How Much Does Long-Term Disability Insurance Cost?" Policygenius, March 16, 2018, https://www.policygenius.com/disability-insurance/learn/how-much-does-long-term-disability-insurance-cost/
4. "Insurance for Your House and Personal Possessions," Insurance Information Institute, https://www.iii.org/article/insurance-for-your-house-and-personal-possessions
5. Colin Lalley, "Employer-Provided Group Life Insurance," Policygenius, February 21, 2019, https://www.policygenius.com/life-insurance/group-life-insurance/
6. Barbara Marquand, "The Differences Between Term and Whole Life Insurance," NerdWallet, April 26, 2019, https://www.nerdwallet.com/blog/insurance/what-is-the-difference-between-term-whole-life-insurance/

264

7. "Plan for Transition: What You Should Know About the Transfer of Brokerage Account Assets on Death," FINRA, June 17, 2015, https://www
.finra.org/investors/alerts/plan-transition-what-you-
should-know-about-transfer-brokerage-account-assets-
death

Part 5: How to Stay the Road and Enjoy the Journey

Chapter 15: Focus on What You Can Control

1. Carol Dweck, *Mindset: The New Psychology of Success* (Ballantine Books
2007), 6–7.
2. March Manson, "Diversify Your Identity," May 14, 2012, https://
markmanson.net/diversify-your-identity
3. *Van Wilder*, film, directed by Walt Becker, performed by Ryan Reynolds,
Myriad Pictures, In-Motion AG Movie & TV Productions, World Media
Fonds V (WMF V), and Tapestry Films, 2002.
4. Laura Vanderkam, *168 Hours: You Have More Time Than You Think* (Portfolio 2011), 34–36.
5. Kai Sato, "Why the 5 People Around You Are Crucial to Your Success," *Entrepreneur*, May 9, 2014, https://www.entrepreneur.com/
article/233444
6. Leif Denti, Isak Barbopuolos, Ida Nilsson, Linda Holmberg, Magdalena
Thulin, Malin Wendeblad, Lisa Anden, and Emelie Davidsson, "Sweden's
Largest Facebook Study," Gothenburg Research Institute, March 6, 2012,
https://gupea.ub.gu.se/handle/2077/28893

1. Bob Proctor, *The Art of Living* (TarcherPerigee 2015), 31.

Index

About the Authors

Roger Ma, CFP® is an award-winning financial planner at lifelaidout, a publisher strategist at Google, and a contributor to *Forbes*. He was named one of *InvestmentNews*'s "40 Under 40" in financial planning in 2017, and one of the top 100 Most Influential Financial Advisors by Investopedia in 2018 and 2019. Roger's personal finance advice has appeared in numerous publications, including Bloomberg, CBS News, CNBC, and the *Washington Post*.

Roger previously worked in investment banking for seven years and holds a Bachelor of Science in Business and Economics from Carnegie Mellon University. Roger lives in New York City with his wife, Jennifer; son, Owen; and two cats, Josie and Junebug.

You can learn more about Roger at `lifelaidout.com`.

Jennifer Ma is a New York City-based writer, editor, and communications professional. Her experience has spanned various communications roles in diverse industries. Jennifer has also served as a contributing writer at a number of finance, travel, and lifestyle publications. She holds a Bachelor of Arts in English from the University of Virginia.

Jennifer is the proud wife of Roger Ma, and the doting mother of their son, Owen (as well as their fur babies, Josie and Junebug, of course).